Contents

Aims

This book reviews the role of daylight in building design and offers practical guidance on the design and position of windows and rooflights. It is based on UK practice and, while meant primarily for architects, will help engineers who wish to extend their understanding of daylight design.

For both architects and engineers it will contribute to Continuing Professional Development. For those who studied Environmental Control or Environmental Science as part of their training, this book should serve as a refresher course. Those with experience in the design of lighting based on solid engineering principles, will find that the perceptual approach adopted here offers an additional set of criteria to consider.

As energy conscious design leads to daylit buildings with controlled supplementary electric light, the architect and the lighting engineer will need to collaborate at the early design stages, and will therefore need to understand each other's concerns.

Learning objectives

When you have completed this book, you should:

- be aware of the main aspects of lighting to be considered when deciding the size, shape, position and detailing of windows;

- be familiar with methods for estimating window areas at an early stage in design, and with techniques for calculating specific daylight factors at later stages;

- understand the circumstances in which electric light should be used in combination with daylight, and the criteria for designing this use of lighting;

- know how to apply the British Standard recommendations for access to sunlight in your designs for new buildings;

- be aware of the main types of sunlight controls, and the geometric parameters for designing them;

- appreciate that daylight can contribute to energy efficiency;

- be familiar with the main published references on daylight design, and with ways of studying the subject further.

Advice to users

This book

A brief introduction to daylighting is followed by *Twenty questions* — an initial test of your current understanding of some aspects of the subject. Do not be disappointed if this quiz reveals gaps in your knowledge.

In practice, the designer has to combine a number of different design aspects into a single whole. With this in mind, the sections following *Twenty questions* cover:

- four examples of buildings in which various design aspects have been successfully combined,

- five key design aspects examined separately in detail: *View, Appearance of interiors, Daylight and skylight, Daylight with electric light,* and *Sunlight,* each followed by a self-assessment exercise (answers towards the end of the book), and

- worked examples and practical exercises for you to practice putting these design aspects together.

The text relates throughout to practice in which the possible variants are numerous. Some of the questions asked are not supplied with answers — they are there to provoke thought and your responses are more important than the authors' opinions.

Prior knowledge

No prior study is required, but we assume you already have a professional qualification in architecture or building services engineering. The introductory document to this series[1] provides information on the basic concepts and terms used in lighting design.

Equipment required

The only equipment required is a pad of paper, a soft pencil or a pen, a scale rule, a calculator and a small knife or scissors.

Essential references

To gain maximum advantage from this book, you will need to get the following essential references.

- *BS 8206:Part 2:1992: Code of practice for daylighting*[2], (referred to in this book as the *BS Daylight Code*).

- *CIBSE Applications manual: Window design*[3] (referred to in this book as the *CIBSE Window manual*)

The reference numbers given above and later in the text refer to the publications listed on page 71.

Introduction

St Dominic's in Rotterdam

Buildings and daylight

Throughout history buildings have provided security, privacy, comfort and shelter. Daylight is an important factor in buildings, it gives illumination for indoor activities and visual links with the outside, and brightens the interior. In respect of daylight, the building envelope can be thought of as a light fitting designed to control the quantity and quality of the light it filters.

Windows

Where rooflights are not available, the depth to which light from the sky can penetrate a building depends on the height of window heads possible within a storey. This can affect the width of a building block and its relationship to adjacent buildings. The sizes, proportions, details and positions of window openings are fundamentally to do with the amount of light entering a building, its distribution and quality. Historically they have been conditioned by the materials and technology available at the time. Windows also greatly influence a building's external appearance.

There is a great variety of window forms and associated effects. These range from the slit windows with wide internal splays in Norman castles, to the ordered repetition of pedimented openings in a Renaissance palace, to the all-glass facade — tinted, sealed and draped — in the city office buildings of this century. See Figures 1–4.

While designers will be influenced by fashion and architectural styles, their primary aim must be to meet human needs, both physical and emotional. The challenge is to relate the need for daylight and sunlight to the design of the space for activities within the building, and to the physical environment needed by its occupants.

1 14th century manor

3 19th century woollen mill

4 20th century office

2 17th century royal palace

Vision and adaptation

The introductory package to this series[1] examines how we see the world about us. Adaptation is a key part of this. The human eye can see well within only a limited range of brightness at any given moment. The range rises and falls continually as we look around, its level being determined by the general level of brightness and, specifically, by the brightest thing in view. This is a mechanism to avoid visual discomfort in daily life and to protect the sensors in the eyes from things that are troublesomely bright. It is most familiar as the adjustment that takes place when we go indoors on a bright day: at first we cannot see well, but our vision rapidly improves as our eyes adapt to the lower levels of light. Also, our attention is given most readily to the best lit thing in view.

An important rule follows from the above — those things that must be clearly seen should be the best lit. Using this rule, environments can be designed to provide good vision at relatively low levels of illumination (thereby saving energy), or to allow the scrutiny of fine detail.

The search for energy efficiency

In recent years greater recognition has been given to the contribution that daylight can make to energy conservation in buildings. At one time it was thought that in a daylit building the loss of heat through windows in winter always represented a net energy debit. But this disregarded the solar heat gain through windows in the heating season and the reduced use of electric lighting throughout the year. Experience has now shown that buildings that are chiefly daylit have lower running costs and are more energy efficient — see Appendix B. This is the case particularly in large buildings such as offices and other workplaces that are occupied during the day. Examples are given in *Energy efficient lighting in buildings*[4].

To achieve daylighting that is both energy efficient and provides comfortable and convenient working conditions requires careful design. Aspects such as controlling glare, sun shading and electric lighting controls are referred to later in this document. They are dealt with more fully in another document in this series[1], *Energy efficiency and lighting design.*

An integrated approach to daylight and electric light, as well as to comfort and energy usage, is needed now more than ever. This calls for close co-operation between architect and engineer. Traditionally, it has been the architect who understood daylight and the engineer who specialised in electric lighting. Now the architect must also appreciate the contribution electric light can make to the interior, while the engineer must also understand the character and quality of daylight the architect is trying to achieve.

Twenty questions

You might like to test your knowledge of daylight. The difficulty of these questions varies and you are not expected to be able to get all the answers right at this stage.

1   Describe three main functions of windows.

2   Distinguish between the terms *daylight, skylight* and *sunlight*.

3   What guidance is available on the form and orientation of a new building on an urban site, which will ensure that sunlight is provided for it and preserved for existing buildings?

4   How do Building Regulations affect the size of glazing areas?

5   Distinguish between *possible* and *probable* sunlight hours.

6   Is the *working plane* for lighting design purposes usually taken as being a horizontal plane 0.7, 0.8 or 0.85 m above floor level?

7   A glossy surface reflects more light than a matt surface of the same reflectance. True or false?

8   Name three factors which contribute to materials deteriorating from exposure to light.

9   On an overcast day, is the southern sky brighter than the northern sky?

10   How do the concepts of *daylight factor* and *average daylight factor* differ? What does each tell you?

11   The average daylight factor recommended for dwellings should be at least 2% in which of the following: bedrooms, living rooms or kitchens?

12   In a daylit office building, the choice of switching controls can reduce the use of lighting by 30–40%. True or false?

13   Name four types of electric lighting control that can be used with daylighting.

14   What aspects would you consider when designing an interior which is to be lit by daylight combined with electric light?

15   When might supplementary electric lighting be needed?

16   Direct and reflected sunlight are included in all values of internal illuminance in skylight calculations. True or false?

17   What is a *window reference point* and how is it used?

18   Should the deepest sun penetration in an interior be expected from the east or from the south?

19   What is the difference between *disability glare* and *discomfort glare*?

20   Is there a legal right to daylight?

Answers on page 61

Four examples of good modern practice

Offices at Wilmslow, Cheshire

House in Victoria Road, Wilmslow, Cheshire

Burrell Collection galleries, Glasgow

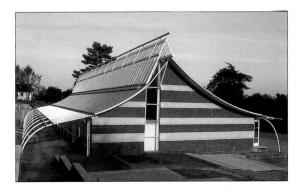

Westgate School, Winchester, Hampshire

An office

**Refuge Assurance plc headquarters
Wilmslow, Cheshire**
Architects: **Building Design
Partnership**

A positive approach to daylight and
view creates a high quality working
environment. This building is wide
but has courtyards and therefore no
workspace is more than 6 m from a
window. Daylight seems dominant.

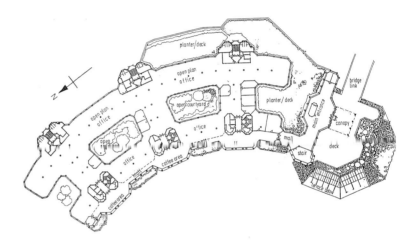

Plan of one of the office floors — level 2

Reception
Gentle and varied patterns of light and
soft-edged shadows with small, sharp
reflections from polished surfaces are in
keeping with the muted colour scheme.
Lighting from the louvred clerestory
balances side lighting from large view
windows.

Sequential use of light
A view from the large uplit office space through the darker lift lobby to the daylit perimeter corridor with a full height view to the landscape beyond.

Flow of light
The waiting area thrusts out southwards into the landscape; with full height windows on three sides it is almost an outdoor room. The flow of light can be deduced from the way in which the lighting models (ie reveals the shape of) the multi-sided bank of seating. Compare the effect of the matt ceiling with that of the mirror ceiling in the coffee area.

Uplighting
Uplighting in large offices can be manually controlled after midday. There is always a pleasant ambience, with interesting patterns of light on the ceiling. Also, effective *contrast grading* (see page 24) prevents glare and harsh silhouetting of the window wall. Manually controlled cavity blinds in the double glazing prevent solar discomfort at perimeter work spaces.

Coffee area
The coffee area below the raised restaurant overlooks a water garden to the north, giving a bright view on a sunny day. The multi-faceted columns are modelled by the bright flow of daylight. The glossy ceiling gives a mirror image of a well lit groundscape, dissolving the ceiling plane and providing contrast grading between indoors and the outside view.

A house

Victoria Road, Wilmslow, Cheshire
Architect: **James Wareham**

Skilful daylighting creates a high
quality environment in a small town
house. View, privacy, skylight and
sunlight have all influenced the
design.

Situated in a small Victorian development, the north facade is simple
and well ordered with banded brickwork matching the houses of the
area. The major windows throughout are tall and have two lights,
those on the south side having greater width for sunlight and for
views of the secluded garden.

Staircase and landing
The staircase leads to a galleried landing giving access to the bedrooms. The view from the half landing shows
how daylight permeates the house. Privacy is provided by net curtains. The pale paintwork reflects light from well
positioned windows to minimise any silhouette effect.

Bedroom

Small windows in gable walls provide cross-lighting which models furniture and relieves shadows on main window walls. The softening effect can be seen here in the principal bedroom where the large eaves act as a sun shield and reduce sky glare. But do the dark-stained timber windows contrast too heavily with the brightness of the view they frame, creating a silhouette effect?

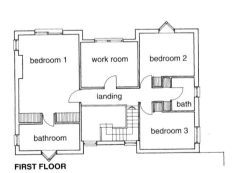

FIRST FLOOR

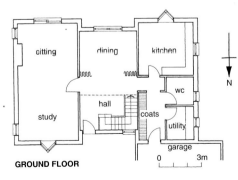

GROUND FLOOR

0   3m

Plan of the house

Entrance hall

The entrance hall carries through the centre of the house to become a dining room with a view out to the garden.

An art gallery

The Burrell Collection, Glasgow
Architect: **Barry Gasson**

This is a parkland gallery with wide-ranging needs for display and presentation. Daylight, grass, trees and other plants provide a context and reflect the relationship between art and nature.

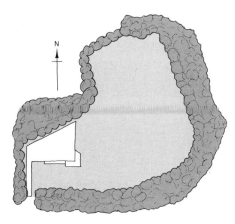

Plan
Sited against a large copse, the gallery gives intimate north and west views into woodland, and from the other aspects open views across parkland. The inter-relationship between daylight, nature and the galleries is a major theme.

Daylit cross-route
Armour is displayed along one of the two daylit cross-routes. The lighting is diffuse, producing shadows — the edges of these are relieved by reflected light from the bright floor and wall surfaces. Sky views are shielded by the louvre effect of the roof timbers and by the density of the woodland view. Daylight can be supplemented by electric lighting from conduits along the roof springing.

Courtyard

The courtyard is flanked by the three principal rooms reproduced from Burrell's Hutton Castle. There is an abundance of natural light from the glazed roof. Sunlight imposes its own patterns on those of the paving and on the sandstone exterior walls.

North gallery

The main perimeter circulation route along the north side provides close contact with the woodland view. The closely spaced structural timbers at clerestory level effectively obstruct oblique sky views so that the emphasis is on interior light. The rooflights from the cross galleries and their end view windows punctuate the route and give varied patterns of light and shade on both floor and columns.

A school

**Westgate School,
Winchester, Hampshire**
Architects: Hampshire County
Architect's office

A recent example from the
Hampshire County Architect's
office in which the cross-section is
generated by the daylighting.

View from the west

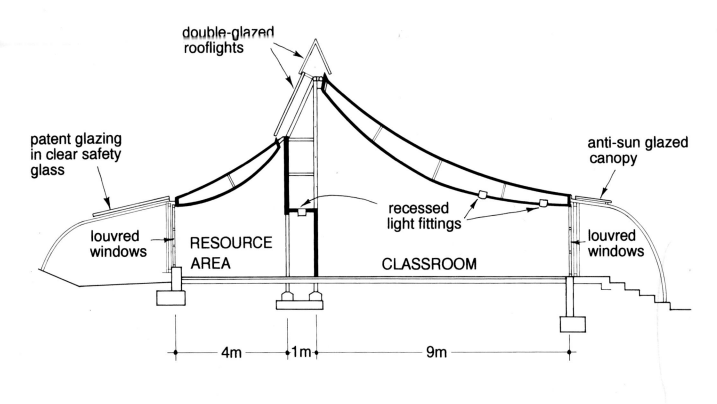

double-glazed
rooflights

patent glazing
in clear safety
glass

anti-sun glazed
canopy

recessed
light fittings

louvred
windows

RESOURCE
AREA

CLASSROOM

louvred
windows

4m   1m   9m

Cross-section
The low external walls on north and south are fully glazed, while external glass canopies reduce glare and
excessive sun. The roof down the spine of the building is glazed, allowing skylight to spill down into the back of
the classrooms and the adjoining resource area. Electric light fittings are recessed and are placed to both
illuminate work areas and brighten building surfaces.

A resource area

One bay in the south wall

View from a classroom up into the rooflight

Key areas in daylight design

The whole and the parts

While the design of daylighting should be viewed as a whole, it is often helpful to consider its different aspects separately. In this book we study five key aspects:

1 **the view out of the building**

2 **the effect of daylight on the appearance of interiors**

3 **daylight and skylight**

4 **combining daylight and electric light**

5 **the treatment of sunlight**

Integrating these aspects is not always straightforward, for example the best views may not be in the direction which gives access to adequate sunlight. The design process may then have to be an iterative one, with various options being examined in turn until the best balance is reached.

Aspects other than lighting

Daylighting has implications beyond lighting itself. These fall outside the scope of this book but some can be mentioned here.

- In many buildings, windows and rooflights are also the chief means of natural ventilation.

- Window size affects heat gain and heat loss.

- External noise levels may restrict the opening of windows, causing overheating if windows are large.

- Glazed areas may present safety problems, for example the risk of injury from accidental breakage.

- Windows need to be accessible to be cleaned conveniently and safely.

- The maintenance of movable equipment such as sun blinds must be considered at the design stage.

- Questions of energy efficiency arise at many points in daylight design, as there is considerable energy-saving potential in daylighting.

Cost considerations

The various daylight options which emerge in the course of design will incur different costs. These must be compared as the design develops, perhaps using discounted cash flow methods to relate capital and running costs. A quantity surveyor will be able to advise on suitable methods (see also BS 8207[5]).

1 View

A room with a view in Grindleton, Lancashire

A room with a view

People like to be able to see out of buildings they use for any length of time, such as their homes or work places. This seems to be true whether the outlook is rolling parkland or a city street, a distant landscape or a back yard. People object when they know there is a view but cannot see out.

What would you say are the main reasons for this desire to see out?

Few people would call themselves claustrophobic, yet no one enjoys being visually enclosed for long. A window allows one to keep in touch with the changing weather and the time of day. It offers a visual rest centre enabling eye muscles to relax on a relatively distant point. It can also assist orientation, helping people in a complex building to find their way around.

This is how the the BS Daylight Code[2] sums it up: *All occupants of a building should have the opportunity for the refreshment and relaxation afforded by a change of scene and focus.* And the Code recommends that: *Unless an activity requires the exclusion of daylight, a view out-of-doors should be provided irrespective of its quality.* (Page 7, clause 4.1)

How can a designer best meet this recommendation? Clearly there will be different requirements in, say, a hospital ward, a reference library, a church, and an office.

How can one make the most of whatever view is available?

Is there a minimum size of window below which people would feel cheated of the view?

5 Two views from the back of a deep room through windows 20% (upper) and 30% (lower) the area of the window wall

Minimum view window

Research has been carried out both on existing buildings and in experiments that allowed observers to adjust the sizes of windows in large scale models. It was found that there is a threshold size below which windows do not provide a sufficient view, depending on how far one is from the window. These critical minimum window sizes are given in Table 1. See also Figure 5.

**Table 1   Minimum glazed areas for view
(when windows are restricted to one wall)**

Maximum depth of room (distance from window wall)	Minimum area of window wall (as seen from inside)
<8m	20%
8-11m	25%
11-14m	30%
>14m	35%

Notes: Windows that are primarily designed for view may not provide adequate illumination for tasks to be done in the room.
Table 1 has been reproduced from page 8 of the *BS Daylight Code*[2].
It also appears as Table B9.1 in the *CIBSE Window manual*[3].

Placing windows

Windows of at least the minimum sizes given above, should be located where occupants, in as many positions as possible in the room, can enjoy a view out. A natural scene, even on quite a small scale, with trees or other plants and sky will be preferred for the variety and movement it offers. Where the outlook is urban and wholly man-made, most people will prefer a view that is dynamic, including the activities of people as well as the changing weather.

View will also be a factor in placing buildings on the site and in positioning rooms in a building, see Figure 6.

6 School kitchen staff enjoy a secluded view

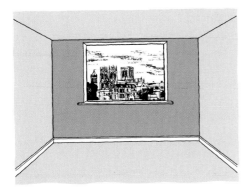

No foreground

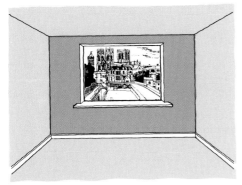

The whole skyline

Some sky

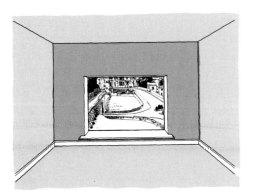

No sky

7 How the same view would look from a given point indoors, with the window at four different heights

(Adapted from the *CIBSE Window manual*[3].)

Analysing views

The *BS Daylight Code*[2] suggests it may be helpful to analyse views in layers. Most unrestricted views have three layers, as follows.

- *Upper* (*distant*) — the sky down to the natural or man-made skyline.
- *Middle* — natural or man-made objects such as fields, trees, hills and buildings.
- *Lower* (*close*) — the foreground, for example plants and paving.

A similar breakdown is illustrated in the *CIBSE Window manual*[3], see Figure 7. Both publications conclude that views which include all three layers are the most satisfying. In practice this is not always possible, but, if taken as an aim from the start of a design, it may be achieved more often than one might at first think. Satisfaction with views is certainly much reduced behind the *no-sky line*, ie where no sky is visible.

Privacy and security

A window that gives a view outside may also allow people to see into the building. This is not always welcome. Blinds or net curtains can often overcome this difficulty, but care is needed in siting sensitive rooms.

Overlooking can be a problem, particularly in high density housing. To some extent this is a cultural matter — in The Netherlands, for example, families do not seem embarrassed to be seen after nightfall through large, uncurtained living-room windows.

While it is not usually possible to see far into a daylit building, when electric lighting is switched on the interior becomes visible. As a general rule, one's level of adaptation is determined by the brightness of the space one is in, and details of other less bright spaces cannot be seen. Do some experimenting in the buildings that you use.

In some circumstances, security and the need to supervise space around buildings may be decisive in the size, shape and position of windows.

Practical trials

You might like to try the practical exercise in the box below.

For this exercise, use a room (or rooms) in buildings known to you — your office or home or a recently completed project you have designed. In each case, the views should be judged from the normal, usually sitting, position of the room's occupants.

1   Can all occupants see through windows that come up to at least the minimum glazed area recommended in the *BS Daylight Code*[2]? How do the views shape up in terms of layers?

Are there any problems connected with privacy?

2   Draw a plan of the room and plot the *no-sky line* on it. (The no-sky line is illustrated in Figure 22 on page 30.) Do any regular users have to work behind this line?

3   As a further exercise, look at the photograph of the view in the *Accessories* through each of the window arrangements which you can mock up using the *window-wall templates*.

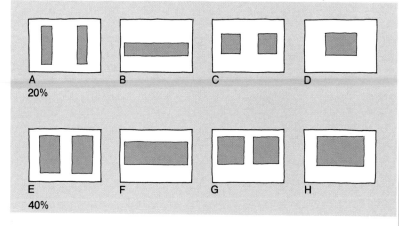

Which of the window arrangements makes the most of the view?

Why? Can you put them in order of preference?

4   Devise some other window arrangements. Keep the same total glazed area and consider various room uses (eg doctor's waiting room, office, living room), bearing in mind the effect of window arrangements on furniture and curtains, and so on.

Note   There is a more detailed exercise on view and other aspects of window design on page 54. It begins by using a pair of scaled L-shaped masks to choose the view and decide the position and size of the window.

Self-assessment exercise 1

1   What are the benefits of having a window with a view? Which do you think is the most important?

2   In rooms with windows in one wall only, why do deeper rooms need larger view windows?

3   How do lace or net curtains affect the views into and out of a room by day and night?

4   What is the minimum view-window area recommended by the *BS Daylight Code*[2] for the room shown below. (The dimensions given are internal.)

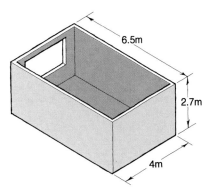

5   You are designing a large office building on a city centre site. The activities housed and the site constraints indicate a multi-storey building and a deep plan. Some people would have to work too far from the external wall for the minimum view window recommendations of the *BS Daylight Code*[2] to be met. How can at least some of the qualities offered by a view out-of-doors be provided within the building?

Answers on page 64

2 Appearance of interiors

8 In this house by Maxwell Fry, warm-coloured walls and low-brightness views out of windows make a restful scene. Reflected light from deep sills and a light ceiling carries deep into the room

When skies are clear the sunlight is direct, giving sharply cut highlights through the windows onto the floor and walls. Contrasts are strong, giving a dramatic effect; colours are enlivened and textures accentuated. Skylight, on the other hand, whether from a clear or overcast sky, is diffuse. Contrasts are reduced, both within a room and between inside and outside. The character is softer and more restful.

Daylighting radically affects the character of an interior. It enhances form, texture and colour. It can help to create feelings of spaciousness or enclosure, calm or excitement. The proportions, detailing and placing of the windows themselves play a key role in interior design.

The sense of brightness is related both to the quantity of light coming directly from the sky and the amount of light reflected from major surfaces. A space with windows in more than one wall, soft shadows and light surface finishes, will feel bright and airy.

Interiors with inadequate skylight from badly disposed windows and dark surfaces with little contrast will appear gloomy. Can you think of examples of spaces in buildings you know well that appear to you to be bright or gloomy? Do the points above explain their different characters or are there other reasons?

Figures 8–10 illustrate good use of daylight in two characteristic houses from the 1930s.

9 Plan of main floor of house in Figure 10
(From *The modern house in England* by F R S Yorke, The Architectural Press, 1944, second edition)

10 In Connell, Ward and Lucas's house, windows on three sides and white walls produce a stimulating, high key interior

The flow of light

11 Entrance gallery, Residenz, Munich

12 Light from side windows modelling the interior and brightening vertical surfaces far from the windows

13 Sparkle from glass, metal and gilding in 18th century Vienna

The main flow of daylight through a side window is predominantly horizontal. It is this characteristic which provides the light for many of the vertical surfaces, even those deep in the room, and brings out the modelling of solid objects — Figure 12. Windows which have heads close to the ceiling give higher light levels towards the back of the room than similar windows set lower in the wall.

If the contrast between highlights and shadows is considerable, the effect will be dramatic (as in Figure 11). If it is too great, the effect may be judged harsh and unpleasant. Where light flows at an oblique angle across a surface it emphasises its texture; the more oblique the angle, the greater the effect. This, however, may also reveal surface defects such as uneven plaster work.

When windows can be placed in other walls as well, the patterns of light and shade will alter and shadows may be softened. But this can go too far, for example if there are large windows in two or three walls and all the surfaces are matt and of high reflectance. In this case the light may be too diffuse, lacking positive direction, and the effect flat and lacking interest. The designer may wish to adjust the relative sizes of the windows, not only to improve the modelling but also to emphasise a particular view or create a sense of directional movement.

Reflecting surfaces which are glossy give bright, mirror-like reflections and can cause dazzle. This can be disturbing on large areas. Conversely, polished metal fittings or gloss paint on architectural trim produce an enlivening sparkle — Figure 13.

Think again of the bright and gloomy (dark) examples you were asked to recall on page 22. Look carefully at the effects of light and shade. Is there any softening of shadows by reflected light; are there interesting textural effects? From certain positions you may see some forms in silhouette or see disturbing reflections. To what extent do these observations help explain your reaction to the appearance of the space?

14 Georgian (late 18th century) window in the library at the Architectural Association, London

Avoiding glare from windows

As you will have seen, the form and placing of windows in a room affect the distribution of light, the pattern of light and shade, and the modelling of forms and textures of surfaces.

A window punched straight through a wall is more likely to cause glare because of the sharp contrast in luminance between the window and the wall. This *silhouette effect* can be reduced by *contrast grading*: designing the surround of the window so that the transition between the bright opening and the relatively dark wall is gradual.

Examples of contrast grading

The typical Georgian window is a good example of refined window design — Figure 14. The head is usually close to the ceiling while the sill is often quite low, reducing the silhouette effect of the wall below with reflected light from the well illuminated floor. Reflections from the floor, and from the ground outside, light up the ceiling above. Deep window reveals, which usually house internal shutters, are often splayed, increasing the effective width of the opening and providing contrast grading to reduce glare from the window. Small window panes are divided by slender tapered glazing bars usually painted white to minimise the silhouette effect, to reduce glare and to make the view out more comfortable.

The principles of contrast grading can be followed in the detailing of windows today, even if window sizes and framing materials may differ — Figure 15.

15 Internal and external views of modern windows at St Anne's College, Oxford

24

Rooflighting

Adding rooflights to an otherwise windowless space can provide some measure of contact with changes in the weather outside. In rooms with side windows, rooflights can modify the overall flow of light so that shadows are softened and walls not receiving direct light from the windows are brightened.

A carefully designed roof lighting system will provide a more even distribution of light than side lighting. A given area of glazing material will transmit more light, the nearer the slope of the glazing is to the horizontal; but more sun will also penetrate. For maximum solar control, the glazing has to be vertical and face due north — the classic *northlight* roof used in many factories. To produce the same daylight factor, a northlight roof will require at least three times as much glass as a shed roof with nearly horizontal rooflights, and the heat loss will be much greater.

In designing rooflights, we need to consider the distribution of light within the room as well as the level of lighting on the horizontal plane. For example, the northlight roof provides a large vertical component, but only from one direction, while the similar *monitor* roof form provides light to the vertical plane from two directions.

Atriums

The atrium is a design strategy that has been used increasingly in recent years. An extensive glassed roof brings daylight into the centre of a large, often multi-storeyed building. The atrium thus acts as a link with the outdoors for parts of the building that would otherwise be wholly internalised and dependent on static electric light. See Figures 16–19 overleaf.

The atrium will generally be at the hub of the building, providing a space for circulation and relaxation. It often contains planting and provides adjacent, and otherwise enclosed, rooms with views. The transition from this well daylit area to adjacent rooms relying on electric light should be treated in the ways described in the section on *Daylight with electric light* (page 36). At night the glazed surfaces will appear either as black or as mirrors of the interior, only becoming transparent where the external illuminance is greater than that inside.

An atrium can produce valuable solar heat gain in winter, but is likely to produce excessive solar heat gain in summer if not shielded against the summer sun. For methods of controlling sunlight, see section 5, page 40.

16 Bentalls, Kingston-upon-Thames

As shown by the buildings in Figures 16 to 19, atriums can bring daylight into multi-storey buildings on deep sites in urban settings, creating an exhilarating sense of space and light. The designer has to consider the gains and losses of energy and the appearance of such large glazed areas after dark. Also, in daytime, the very bright 'ceiling' overhead may make the floor — several storeys below — seem gloomy in contrast, even though the level of daylight there is adequate. Each of the buildings shown succeeds in dealing with these problems and is worth a visit.

17 Harlequin Centre, Watford

18 The Ark, Hammersmith, London

19 St Enoch Centre, Glasgow

Self-assessment exercise 2

1   A room is provided with textured wall surfaces. It is lit by windows on the front wall only. Would the texture appear to be most pronounced:

  - near the window?
  - towards the rear of the side walls?
  - on the rear wall?

2   What should be the form of a window if maximum penetration to the rear of the room is required?

3   What is the effect on the appearance of an interior of introducing a secondary window in a wall at right angles to the main window wall?

4   How can the design of a window and its surrounds contribute to the quality of lighting in a room by reducing glare?

5   Can models be used to assess the effect of different window arrangements?

Answers on page 65

3 Daylight and skylight

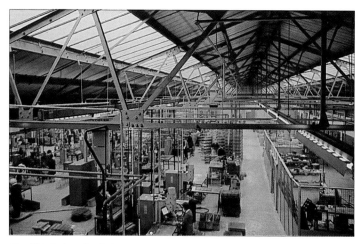

Daylit interior of a factory

Light for daytime work

The light in which people work — whether at a desk, an assembly line, a laboratory bench or darning socks at home — needs to be of good quality as well as sufficient in quantity.

Daylight has qualities that can make work easier, as well as creating enjoyable interiors with variety in brightness and the refreshment and relaxation of a view outside. Side windows (and rooflights in some situations) provide directional light which gives good three-dimensional modelling for tasks. Also, the appearance daylight gives to colours is considered excellent for most purposes.

Where one can take work to a window, the level of illumination provided by skylight — let alone sunlight — cannot easily be matched. In the 18th century, attics in the houses of weavers who worked at home had continuous strip windows; people making lace by hand worked outdoors when they could.

But daylight is variable, and in poor weather, or at the ends of the working day, even a building that is generously daylit may need a top up of electric light. Furthermore, buildings that require a deep plan form because of the activities they house or site constraints, or because of external obstructions to daylight, are likely to need a substantial supplement of electric lighting during the day. For these purposes it is not enough just to switch on the after-dark lighting.

To get the best and most economical results, the design of daylighting and the electric lighting must be considered jointly, with the architect and lighting engineer working together from an early stage. This is the subject of section 4.

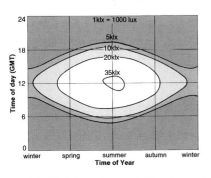

20 Variation of daylight illuminance by time of year and time of day

Table 2 Reflectance of surfaces

Average reflectance

For calculating *average daylight factor,* use R=0.5 for a room with light surfaces, and R=0.3 for a room with darker surfaces.

For other cases, see *BS Daylight Code[2]* p 27.

Some typical reflectances

White ceilings	0.7
Pale walls	0.5
Floors and furniture	0.3
The ground outside	0.1

Obstructions such as buildings are usually assumed to be 20% as bright as the sky behind them.

Source: BS Daylight Code[2] p 27, Table 4.

Deterioration factor

Values for interior surfaces need to be further reduced to allow for deterioration with age and dirt.

For an office in a clean location, the *deterioration factor* may be 0.9, but for dirty work in a dirty location it may be as low as 0.6.

Source: BS Daylight Code[2] p 28, Table 5.

Defining daylight

The new use of the term skylight

All daylight comes from the sun, whether we see it as sunbeams or as the light from a clouded sky. However, for the purpose of calculating the light available for illuminating our work during the day, the source used is the overcast sky. This is now termed *skylight* (not daylight, as before), and is formally defined on page 82.

The internationally accepted standard used as a base for skylight studies is the *CIE overcast sky*. This sky is three times as bright at the zenith (overhead) as at the horizon, and no brighter to the south than to the north. It is assumed that its minimum illumination is 5000 lux outdoors. This figure is exceeded for 85% of the normal working day, averaged throughout the year — see Figure 20. So the CIE overcast sky represents a dull day.

Daylight factor

As daylight levels vary over a large range even on an overcast day, illuminance indoors coming from skylight is, in practice, measured as a ratio. This ratio (*daylight factor*) is the illuminance at a point indoors, usually on the working plane, expressed as a percentage of the illuminance outdoors. So if the illuminance outdoors is 5000 lux, that of a dull overcast sky, a daylight factor of 2% at a point indoors will give an illuminance of 100 lux at that point (2% of 5000 lux = 100 lux).

Figure 21 shows the main components of the skylight which reaches a desk at the back of a room. First there is the direct light from any part of the sky which is visible from the desk. All the other light which reaches the desk is reflected, either outside or inside or both.

Reflected light makes a significant contribution to the working light indoors, the proportion increasing as one moves further from the window. If obstructions, such as buildings opposite, obscure the view of the sky further back in the room, reflected light provides all the illuminance behind the *no-sky line* (defined in Figure 22 overleaf).

As the ceiling and walls form a large part of the internal surface of a room, using light colours can greatly increase reflected light. A light floor finish close to the window can also help, as it reflects direct light from high in the sky. The amount of light reflected depends on the *reflectance* of the surfaces — see Table 2 for some typical values.

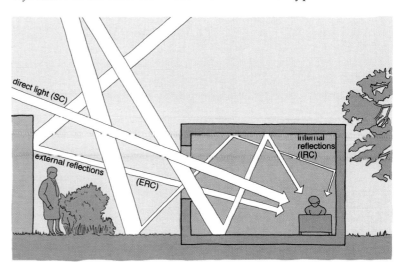

21 The main components of skylight. The desk in this room receives some light directly from the overcast sky. But all the rest is reflected, either outside or inside or both

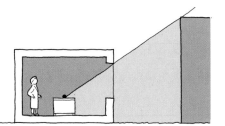

22 The no-sky line rule of thumb: occupants will judge skylight unsatisfactory in those parts of a room where they cannot see the sky — that is, behind the no-sky line

Predicting skylight in design

The no-sky line rule of thumb

The rule in Figure 22 can be used to predict roughly whether a room can be lit by skylight.

Try out this rule of thumb in a selection of interiors known to you:

- in a working interior lit by skylight only, select a series of positions where you consider the illumination on the working plane is not adequate for sustained work, and mark these on a plan of the room;
- now plot points on the plan where the sky cannot be seen from the working plane itself — if you join these points on a plan of the room, you have constructed the no-sky line.

How nearly do these lines coincide? Are they close enough for you to have faith in this rule of thumb?

Average daylight factor

Another broad measure for assessing the adequacy of skylight during the early stages in design is the *average daylight factor*. This is the mean daylight factor in a room over the horizontal working plane.

The formula in Figure 23 below, is used to calculate average daylight factor for windows and rooflights. Tables 3, 4, and 5 give a selection of data from the *BS Daylight Code*[2] for use in the formula. Note in Table 3 that single glazing transmits more light than double glazing, and far more than most tinted and reflective glazing.

By inspecting the formula we can see what influences its value. The daylight factor will be greater if:

- the window is large in proportion to all the surfaces inside the room on which its light is spread, that is if W/A is large,
- the window is clean and transparent, that is if T is large,
- a large angle of open sky can be seen from the window, that is if Θ is large (see Figure 23),
- the internal surfaces of the room are light, that is if R is large.

Visible sky angle (Θ)

$$\overline{D} = \frac{W}{A} \frac{T\Theta}{(1 - R^2)}$$

where:

$\overline{D}$ = average daylight factor

W = window area in m² (using Table 5 to correct for framing)

A = area of all surfaces of the room in m² (floor, ceiling, and walls including windows)

T = glass transmittance (from Table 3) corrected for dirt (using Table 4)

Θ = visible sky angle, in degrees

R = average reflectance of area A (from Table 2)

23 The *average daylight factor*

Table 3 Transmittance of glazing

Type of glazing	Trans- mittance	Area needed	
Single	0.80	□	100%
Double	0.65	□	125%
Triple	0.55	□	140%
Tinted*	0.39-0.66	□⫏	120-210%
Reflective†	0.15-0.26	▭▭⫏	310-530%

For other cases, see *BS Daylight Code*[2], p 28, Table 6
* body-tinted single
† double with one pane clear

Table 4 Dirt correction factors

Type of location	Angle of glazing		
	▮	⬛	▬
Clean	0.9	0.8	0.7
Industrial	0.7	0.6	0.5
Very dirty	0.6	0.5	0.4

Source: *BS Daylight Code*[2], p 28, Table 7

Table 5 Correction for frames

Type of window	Typical correction factor
Metal patent glazing	0.9
Metal frame: large pane	0.8
Wood frame: large pane	0.7
Wood frame: small pane	0.6

For other cases, see *BS Daylight Code*[2], p 28, Table 8

Average daylight factor can be used to calculate the gross area of windows needed when designing a new building. Or, it can be calculated for the windows of an existing building as part of a survey. Tables 6 and 7 list some minimum values of average daylight factor recommended on page 9 of the *BS Daylight Code*[2], for where a predominantly daylit appearance is wanted. These minimum values do not provide a given *quantity* of illumination — this will vary during the day. But they ensure a given ratio between the illumination indoors and outdoors, avoiding excessive contrast between the interior and the view outside.

Table 6 Average daylight factors to give a daylit appearance

Condition	Minimum average daylight factor
Mainly daylit	5%
With supplementary electric lighting	2%

Table 7 Average daylight factors in dwellings*

Type of room	Minimum average daylight factor
Kitchen	2%
Living room	1.5%
Bedroom	1%

*Even if a daylit appearance is not required

Limits to the depth of a room

Even if the average daylight factor for a room meets the minimum specified in Tables 6 and 7, the room may still be too deep (from front to back) to be successfully daylit. A room will be lighter at the back if the following conditions are met:

- its depth is not much greater than its width,
- its depth is not too many times the height of the window head above the floor,
- the surfaces at the back of the room are light.

These factors are taken into account in the *limiting depth rule* given in Figure 24 below.

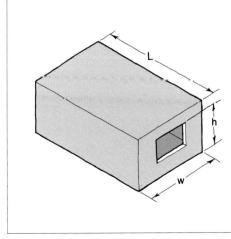

To be successfully daylit from one side, the depth (L) of the room should be limited to meet the following condition:

$$\frac{L}{w} + \frac{L}{h} \leq \frac{2}{(1 - R_b)}$$

where:

L = depth of room from window to back wall

w = width of room measured across the window wall

h = height of window head above floor

R_b = area-weighted average reflectance in the back half of the room (the value for a typical office is likely to be around 0.5)

Source: *BS Daylight Code*[2], p 19

24 The *limiting depth rule*

Positioning the window

How does the height of a window on a wall affect the light it gives?

Figures 25 and 26 consider the effect on the daylight factor of varying the vertical position of a horizontal window in a small office with an unobstructed view. Broadly speaking, the higher up the window is placed, the greater the daylight factor will be. This is because the light from a higher window comes from a higher and therefore brighter part of the sky, and it reaches the desk at a steeper angle. If there were obstructions such as buildings opposite, raising the window would increase the daylight factor even more because more sky would be visible.

But raising the ceiling, so that the same window can be placed higher, will not improve the daylight factor indefinitely. Figure 27 shows the position of the window which maximises the light at the back desk. This occurs when the angle at which the window is seen from the viewpoint is around 45°. No one would normally choose to place a window in this absurd position.

Turning the same window round into a vertical position results in a good design — see Figure 28. As the window head is high, plenty of light gets in, and it is more likely that the view will include sky. Also the low sill improves the chance that seated as well as standing people will get a view of the foreground too.

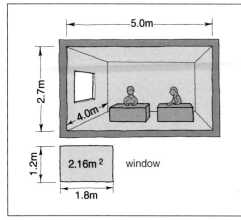

The room
The room is a small office. The area of the window is 20% of the window wall. The view is unobstructed.

The components of daylight factor
The *sky component* (SC) causes all of the variation in daylight factor as we change the height of the window on the wall. As there are no obstructions to the view, there is no *externally reflected component* (ERC). Assuming typical values for the reflective surfaces, the *internally reflected component* (IRC) is 0.7% at the desk in the middle of the room — similar to the average IRC for the whole room. At the back of the room the IRC is lower — 0.5%.

25 The room used for the analysis in Figures 26–28

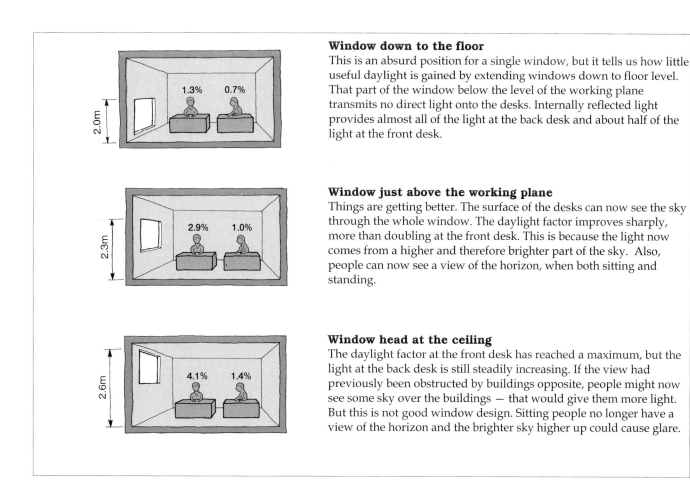

Window down to the floor
This is an absurd position for a single window, but it tells us how little useful daylight is gained by extending windows down to floor level. That part of the window below the level of the working plane transmits no direct light onto the desks. Internally reflected light provides almost all of the light at the back desk and about half of the light at the front desk.

Window just above the working plane
Things are getting better. The surface of the desks can now see the sky through the whole window. The daylight factor improves sharply, more than doubling at the front desk. This is because the light now comes from a higher and therefore brighter part of the sky. Also, people can now see a view of the horizon, when both sitting and standing.

Window head at the ceiling
The daylight factor at the front desk has reached a maximum, but the light at the back desk is still steadily increasing. If the view had previously been obstructed by buildings opposite, people might now see some sky over the buildings — that would give them more light. But this is not good window design. Sitting people no longer have a view of the horizon and the brighter sky higher up could cause glare.

26 Effect of the height of the window head on the daylight factor. A higher window provides more skylight, especially at the back of the room. But sitting people may lose their view. For details of the room and the conditions see Figure 25

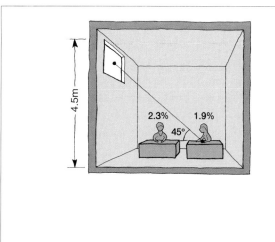

A high window in a taller room
This is another absurd case, but it shows the value of tall windows in deep high rooms. The window is at the level which maximises the light at the back desk. But light at the front desk has dropped below the peak it approached in the third case in Figure 26. Light reaches this front desk from a higher and therefore brighter part of the sky, and at a steeper angle. But, as the window is now further away from the desk, and as it is seen by the desk at a more oblique angle, the direct light reaching the desk now comes from a smaller patch of sky. The internally reflected light is also slightly reduced, as the same amount of incoming light is now spread over a larger surface area.

(The thickness of the wall will further reduce the depth of the window which is visible — an aspect neglected in our analysis. If the wall is thick, this effect can be large.)

27 Raising the window does not improve the skylight indefinitely. The daylight factor reaches a peak when the window is seen from the viewpoint at a vertical angle of about 45°, and drops off rapidly before 60°

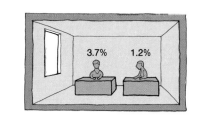

Vertical window
Here, the window shown in Figures 26 and 27 is turned to be vertical and now spans from working plane to ceiling. This window has the advantages of the second and third windows in Figure 26 above, without their disadvantages. Much more direct light comes in the top half of the window than the bottom half, especially in the case of the back desk. The vertical window also transforms the view, improving the chances of including sky and foreground.

28 More light comes through the top than the bottom of a vertical window

Minimum daylight factor

Average daylight factor is only an initial check on the area of glazing to use. It takes no account of the shape or position of the window, and tells us nothing about the distribution of light in a room. For example, the average daylight factor calculated by the formula on page 30 is the same for every window position described in Figure 26, even for the window at floor level.

To make a more accurate check on daylight, it is sometimes necessary, at a later stage in design, to estimate the *minimum daylight factor* at a point in the interior.

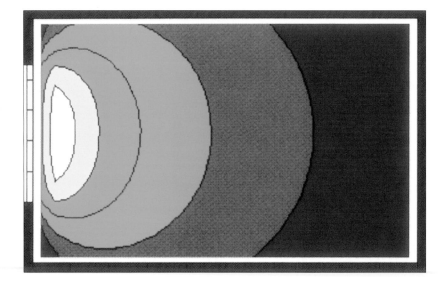

29 Daylight factor contours — produced by the Anglia DAYLIGHT program

There are computer programs that draw contours of daylight factor (see Figure 29) for rooms with common shapes, which may have simple obstructions outside the window. The designer enters the characteristics of the room and windows, and explores the effect on the contours of changing the size and pattern of the windows and other features of the room.

BRE has recently carried out a survey for the Energy Technology Support Unit (ETSU) of the methods used by some 60 architects, planners and lighting specialists to predict daylight (*Daylight prediction methods: a survey of their use*, 1994, available free from ETSU (Harwell Laboratories, Oxfordshire, OX11 0RA). The report lists the names and sources of some 10 daylight programs of UK origin, and a rather larger number of foreign origin, mainly from the USA. The survey revealed that two simple programs for the interior calculations of daylight were used fairly widely, and that the many other more sophisticated programs were used by few of the respondents. A depressing finding of the survey was that almost half of the 33 architects in the survey never made any predictions of interior daylight, and few of those that did used computer programs.

A manual method of calculating daylight factor, using the *pepperpot diagram* in Figure 30, is described in the *Window design exercise* — see page 54. Procedures for calculating daylight factors using daylight protractors, for either windows or rooflights, are given on page 20 of the *BS Daylight Code*[2], and page 26 of the *CIBSE Window manual*[3].

The method of calculation used should make allowance for the transmittance of the glazing, taking account of framing and dirt (Tables 3–5).

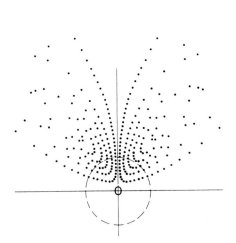

30 The pepperpot diagram

Self-assessment exercise 3

1 What are the main contributions daylight can make to a working interior?

2 Explain the no-sky line concept and give an example of its significance.

3 How is the quantity of skylight at a specific point in the interior expressed?

4 How can glare from windows be minimised?

5 The existing window in the small office shown below has an area of single glazing within the frame that is 20% of the window wall. This is the minimum area the *BS Daylight Code*[2] recommends for view windows for rooms up to 8 m deep. There are no obstructions outside.

- What is the average daylight factor?

- What is the implication for the use of electric lighting?

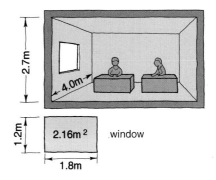

6 Check the same room against the limiting depth rule. The window is low on the wall; its head 0.7 m below the ceiling.

7 If the same room had a larger single glazed window that was 35% of the window wall area, what would the average daylight factor be?

If this larger window was double glazed, to what value would the average daylight factor drop?

8 What area of double glazing would be needed to give an average daylight factor of 5% in this same room?

Sketch the window on the window wall, so as to give good light and view.

Answers on page 66

4 Daylight with electric light

Deep side-lit staff restaurant with electric lighting furthest from window

Most people say they prefer to work by daylight alone, yet many of our workplaces have the electric lights on for much of the day. Perhaps this supplementary electric lighting improves the distribution of working light throughout the room. Or maybe it is just more pleasant. It may even be that the lights are switched on by the cleaners, and we don't like the change brought about by switching them off. Or perhaps we don't even notice that the lights are still on.

You could try the effect of switching off individual lights in the office, or at home, during poor daylighting to see which are the essential ones. The *haystack* provided in the *Accessories* at the back of this book may help you to study modelling effects.

- Does a table lamp near the window, where it may brighten the window wall, have a better effect than the same lamp placed away from the window where it may brighten a gloomy corner?
- Does moving the lamp have more effect on the illumination of the horizontal or vertical surfaces?
- Is the change of colour introduced by electric lighting for better or worse?

It is helpful to know why we want supplementary lighting so that we can provide the appropriate types of electric lighting. The *BS Daylight Code*[2] identifies two specific roles of supplementary lighting:

- *to enhance the overall appearance of the room by improving the distribution of illuminance and by reducing the contrast in luminance between the interior and the view outside,*
- *to achieve satisfactory illuminance on visual tasks.*

Night-time electric lighting

All too often, electric lighting is designed for the night-time condition, although in many instances its main use will be during the hours of daylight. Such schemes will normally be designed to the *CIBSE Code for interior lighting*[6].

Daytime electric lighting

The *CIBSE Window manual* suggests that *When the average daylight factor is less than 2%, the interior will not be perceived as well daylit, and electric lighting may be in constant use* (page 15, para A2.2.31)[3]. If the average daylight factor is between 2% and 5%, electric lighting will be required to supplement and complement the daylight.

For task lighting, the total illuminance from the supplementary electric lighting and daylight should reach the levels required after dark. To limit, for the sake of visual comfort, the contrast between the room interior and the sky, the *BS Daylight Code* (page 11, clause 7.2.4)[2] recommends that the illuminance from the electric lighting should not be less than 300 lux on the working plane. The optimum balance is achieved, the code suggests, when the electric lighting *in areas remote from the windows is approximately the same as the daylight illuminance 2 m from the window.* (But, as daylight levels are constantly varying, this could only be achieved precisely in practice by varying the level of the electric lighting as the daylight varies.) In many instances, the illuminance provided by the night-time lighting will be found to be appropriate. All references to illuminance relate to the horizontal working plane.

Therefore, in working areas, switching on the night-time lighting to provide supplementary lighting over the parts of the room furthest from the window will improve both the quantity of task lighting and the visual comfort found in the interior. Electric lighting to the rest of the room may not be needed. The different directions in which light flows from daylight and artificial light sources may improve the modelling in the rear of the room and serve to lessen shadows produced by one source alone.

Lamp colour

The colour of electric light sources is described by two terms: colour appearance and colour rendering.

Colour appearance of lamps

Because of the variation in the quality of daylight throughout the day, it will not be possible to select an electric light source with an appearance that matches the full range of daylight. The *BS Daylight Code*[2] suggests that these discrepancies may be reduced by:

- using lamps of Intermediate class correlated colour temperature (see BS 8206: Part 1)[7],

- screening lamps from the view of occupants for this purpose; louvres with a cut-off at 45° to the horizontal are preferable to any form of translucent diffuser.

Intermediate class colour appearance means lamps with colour temperatures that are neither *warm* nor *cool* and will be within the band 3300 K to 5300 K. Typical fluorescent lamps are called *white*, often followed by the colour temperature, eg multi-phosphor lamps of 4000 K colour temperature. This class includes metal halide lamps, but not tungsten filament or sodium lamps.

Colour rendering of surfaces and materials

Introducing electric light to a daylit interior can change the appearance of the colours and materials of surfaces. This calls for care, not only in the design of windows and the choices of lamp, but also the choice of colours for surfaces.

Visual tasks which entail accurately recognising colours are best daylit with light from the north sky. There is nothing magical about north skylight, except that during the normal working day it will not include sunlight which would make it variable. Fluorescent tubes, namely multi-phosphor lamps with a *Colour rendering index* greater than 85, have been developed to match the particular spectrum of north skylight closely. These will minimise any shift in the colour appearance of the task as skylight fades.

Electric lighting controls

Controlling electric lighting by switching will not only help to balance daylight and provide working light, but can also cut electricity costs. Surveys by BRE have shown that the use of an appropriate system of control for electric lighting can make a substantial difference to the electricity bill. For example, a 30% to 40% reduction in lighting use in a conventionally daylit commercial building can be achieved. Four basic forms of light control are listed in the *BS Daylight Code* on page 13 (para 9.4)[2]:

a   *manual*
b   *timed switch off, with optional manual reset*
c   *photoelectric switching on/off*
d   *photoelectric dimming*

The choice of the method of control will depend upon the type of occupancy and hours of use. The *CIBSE Window manual*'s Figure A4.1[3] offers the procedure redrawn in Figure 31.

Further information on controls is available in BS 8206: Part 1[7] and in BRE Digest 272[8]. The subject is also covered in greater depth in the *Designing electric lighting in buildings* document in this series[1].

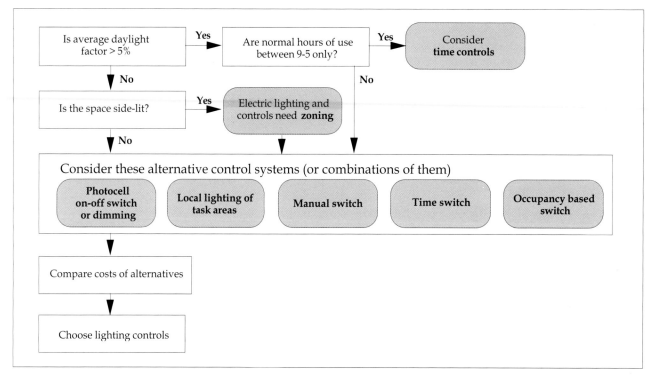

31   Choosing a method for controlling electric light

Self-assessment exercise 4

1   When should a work room be considered as being lit, during the day, by electric light alone?

2   Lamps with which characteristics are appropriately used in conjunction with daylight?

3   How would you arrange the pattern of linear fluorescent fittings in a deep side-lit office with an average daylight factor of 3.5%? How may they be switched off to best effect?

Answers on page 69

5 Sunlight

Effects of sunlight

In this country sunlight is welcomed into most interiors unless there are particular reasons for excluding it. Why do we like sunlight in our buildings?

- Is it because of the increased illumination?
- Are we stimulated by the variability and changing patterns introduced by sunlight?
- Is it because sunlight enlivens colours in the room? It is said that direct sunlight increases the chroma intensity of colours by two steps on the Munsell scale.
- Does it matter that the presence of sunlight comparatively reduces the relative brightness of other things in the room?
- What are the limits to the acceptability of sunlight?

Once we know why we like to admit sunlight into our buildings, we can plan to let it into the spaces that will benefit the most.

Figures 32 and 33 (and also 34 opposite) illustrate buildings where sunlight makes a contribution to the design.

32 Although venetian blinds are provided in the south-facing stairway, the occupants of these offices in Winchester prefer to have the sun flooding in through the full-height windows which also offer generous views of the hill beyond the city

33 In this domestic conversion, the paired window and rooflight face north, the rooflight catching the early morning sun in summer. A smaller window to the south lightens the shadows. Behind the photographer, a large window looks west to a spacious view across the open common. The golden carpet is almost a source of illumination in itself, filling the room with warm reflected light

34 Midwinter sunshine

Sunlight and site layout

When a new building is erected on a site, it should:

- allow adequate skylight and sunlight to reach existing or possible future adjacent buildings, and

- ensure that the new building itself has adequate skylight, sunlight and view (see the extract from the *BS Daylight Code* below)[2].

Rule of thumb

A rule of thumb for checking that sunlight is adequate is given in Figure 35.

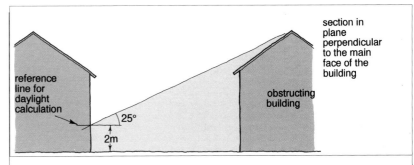

A window will satisfy the sunlight recommendation in the *BS Daylight Code*[2] (see below) if the window wall faces within 90° of due south and no obstruction — measured in the section perpendicular to the window wall — subtends an angle of more than 25° to the horizontal. (Obstructions within 90° of due north of the reference point need not count here.)

35 Rule of thumb for probable sunlight hours

Typical design tasks to which this rule of thumb can be applied are illustrated in Figures 36–38.

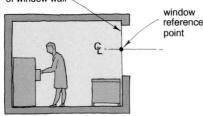

36 Preparing a site layout in a scheme containing more than one building, including deciding the distance of a new building from an existing one

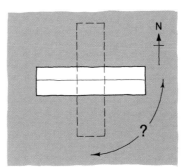

37 Orientating a new building so that a large enough proportion of probable sunlight hours reaches given faces of the building

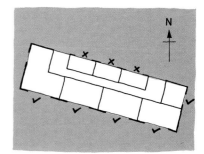

38 Deciding the position within a building of rooms in which the occupants have a reasonable expectation of direct sunlight

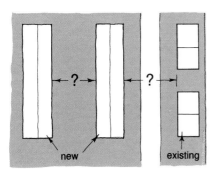

39 The window reference point — definition: the point in the centre of a window (or rooflight) on the plane of the inside surface of the window wall or roof

British Standard recommendations

The *BS Daylight Code* (page 8, clause 5.3)[2] recommends that:
Interiors in which occupants have a reasonable expectation of direct sunlight should receive at least 25% of probable sunlight hours [defined on page 82 of this book]. *At least 5% of probable sunlight hours should be received during the winter months, between 23 September and 21 March. Sunlight is taken to enter an interior when it reaches one or more window reference points* (defined in Figure 39).

A fuller procedure for calculating the percentage of sunlight hours reaching a window reference point in buildings with various orientations is given in the *BS Daylight Code* (page 17, clause 12.2)[2].

Controlling sunlight

Sunlight is welcome, but one can have too much of a good thing. The principle given in the BS Daylight Code (page 8, clause 5.2)[2] is that sunlight should be admitted unless it is likely to cause thermal or visual discomfort to the users, or deterioration of materials.
The Code adds a warning that: *In many buildings, discomfort and overheating may occur if the annual penetration of sunlight exceeds one-third of probable sunlight hours.*

Controls are therefore necessary, particularly in working interiors where people cannot move their work readily. The methods chosen should take account of our variable weather conditions and the fact that, in winter, sun is often desired to brighten and warm interiors, see Figures 40 and 41.

When choosing methods of control, bear in mind the other purposes which windows serve, such as allowing a view out and providing directional light across rooms. The best way of making use of the sun's heat to save energy is described in another document in this series[1], *Energy efficiency and lighting design.*

40 The courtyard of this 19th century hospital building was roofed in glass to provide additional accommodation. South-facing glazing on the upper floor is shielded with fixed louvres which protect working areas from the sun in the summer but admit it in winter (as in this photograph) when it is welcome and provides an energy bonus

41 In these offices in Swindon, energy conservation considerations have led to a naturally ventilated building. Solar heat gain is controlled by a combination of fixed louvres and automatic external roller blinds. When daylight fades, energy-efficient uplighters provide general illumination, supplemented by desk-mounted task lights

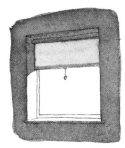

42 Roller blind

43 Venetian blind

44 Retractable awning

45 Overhanging roof

46 Fixed baffle

Methods of control

In this country, adjustable or retractable types of curtains, blinds or shades are often the most appropriate methods to use. In countries further south, with hotter climates and high altitude sun, different techniques of sun shading are needed.

Internal blinds

The most common methods of sun control are simple draw curtains, roller blinds and venetian blinds — Figures 42 and 43. These can be drawn or lowered when needed. They are reasonably easy to use, though venetian blinds need cleaning and maintenance to keep them in good condition, and users may need instructions on how to use them. Choose the colour with care: pure white translucent blinds in full sun can themselves become a source of glare. A blind which is brightly coloured may colour the light in the room.

Try experimenting with a range of materials fixed against a window on a sunny day. The samples should be at least 1 m square; to judge them you should look at them from a distance of about 1 m.

Curtains and internal blinds will prevent the sun's rays from falling on people, desks and delicate fabrics, but the greenhouse effect means that the room will still heat up, perhaps uncomfortably. In winter this can reduce space heating requirements, but in summer it will increase the cooling load in air-conditioned buildings.

External shading

The most effective way of reducing unwanted solar heat gain is by the use of shading devices mounted externally, see Figures 44–46. These methods will also reduce skylight throughout the year, and fixed external screens will therefore need larger glazed areas for a given daylight factor inside the building. External blinds and awnings which can be retracted do not have this problem, but do need to be robust and resistant to wind damage. Some types with open-weave plastic blind material, which are framed so they can project like a shop awning to permit a view under them, have proved reasonably satisfactory in use.

Overhanging roofs, balconies and projecting edge beams (as in BRE's low-energy building) or floor slabs can sometimes be used to provide permanent sun shading. In rehabilitating buildings which have excessive glazed areas, fixed arrays of baffles or fins — or both — have been employed for the same purpose.

The effect of all these methods on daylight factors, and on sun penetration, can be found using the methods discussed in this book. The formula given on page 30 for calculating the average daylight factor can be used to discover the effects of, say, reducing the angle of clear sky visible (or of changes in the glass transmission factor). See also the *Window design exercise* on page 54.

An annotated list of shading devices is given in section B12 of the *CIBSE Window manual*[3].

Solar control glazing

The third method of sun control is to use low transmission glazing in place of normal clear window glass. Glasses made for this purpose are available in two main categories, heat absorbing and heat reflecting. A representative list is given in a table in the *CIBSE Window manual* (Table B5.1, p 40, 41)[3]. Manufacturers of glasses not listed should, for comparison, be asked to give the performance of their product in terms of the categories used in that table.

Solar glasses reduce the transmission of both light and heat, although those in the heat-absorbing category will warm up and re-radiate some heat into the room. Very few glasses reduce heat more than light, but even glass with the lowest light transmission is unlikely to reduce glare from the sun significantly. This is because of the sun's extremely high intensity in contrast with the brightness of surfaces in the room. This contrast will remain despite using a glass with lower transmission.

All solar glasses colour the incoming light. This will rarely be noticed unless different types of glass are mixed in one locality, or the scene outdoors is viewed through an open window or door.

Note that opal or near-white glass, and some patterned glasses and glass bricks, can cause glare indoors in full sun. Blinds will still be needed. Test large samples visually.

Sunlight can fade materials

Many materials become degraded when exposed to light, especially to sunlight, as we know from the way curtains can fade in sunny rooms at home. Three factors affect this: the spectral composition of the light, the illuminance, and the period of exposure. For more about this, see the *BS Daylight Code*[2] on page 14, Section 10, *Conservation of materials inside buildings.*

Predicting sun penetration

Models and mock ups

Fixed external sun shading devices can be costly, and when designing extensive installations of these it might be worth making detailed small-scale models (Figure 47), or even a full-scale mock-up of a sample section. Artificial skies in which small-scale models can be assessed are available at some research stations and teaching institutions (a list of these is given on page 79). For shading tests, an artificial sun is used. Apparatus, such as a heliodon, for predicting the movement of the sun is also likely to be available. A miniature version inside a matchbox was devised by J Lynes.

While sun penetration can be determined geometrically by these methods, the effect of external shading devices on the appearance of an interior cannot. Some form of three-dimensional experiment which you can look into, with as much realistic detail as possible on view, is advisable. You might like to make some simple trials yourself, using the shoebox model described on page 50.

47 Model of classroom in artificial sky used to measure daylight factors in the room and the effect of changing reflection factors of internal surfaces

Computer programs

If you cannot justify the expense of building and testing a model, computer programs may be available to help you predict sun penetration (see page 34).

Sun path diagrams

If no suitable computer program is available, you can use sun path diagrams to predict sun penetration manually.

There are several kinds of sun path diagram, which use different methods of projection for presenting the three-dimensional heavens on a two-dimensional diagram. The most straightforward sun path diagram is perhaps the *equiangular projection* illustrated in Figure 48. It shows the altitude and bearing of the sun at any time of day in any month of the year. You could use this diagram, for example, when doing a drawing to predict where the shadow of a building will fall, or how far the sun will penetrate into a room.

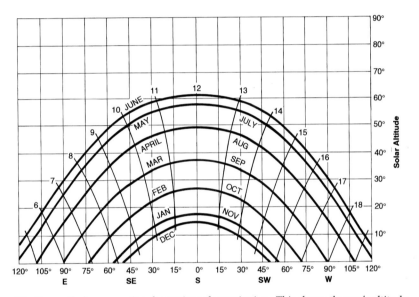

48 Sun path diagram using the equiangular projection. This shows the sun's altitude on the y-axis, and solar azimuth (horizontal bearing) on the x-axis, for different times of year. Time of day is shown by the almost vertical curves. This diagram is for latitude 52° north, just north of London

(Source: **Robins C L**. *Daylighting design and analysis*. Reinhad & Co, New York, 1986)

Some other methods of projection require you to transform the shape of the window before superimposing it on the sun path diagram, for example the *stereographic projection* (described in the *CIBSE Window manual* page 32)[3]. Other methods present sun paths on a circular plan view.

Figure 49 shows a sun path diagram which uses the gnomonic projection (pronounced with a silent g as in gnome). This method allows you to measure sun penetration directly, by superimposing the diagram on a normal elevation of the window.

Later we use the sunpath diagram in Figure 49 to design a canopy to exclude the sun from a chosen position in a room between April and August. A full set of diagrams has separate sheets for different orientations of room, and there are different sets for different latitudes.

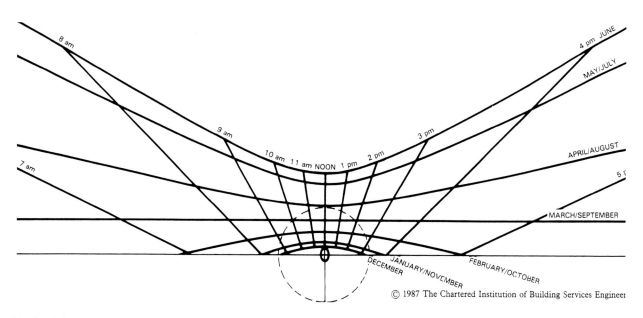

49 South-facing sun path diagram using the gnomonic projection (reduced in size here)

The sun path diagram in Figure 49 is for latitude 53° north in the Midlands. The curves are the paths of the sun one could draw on a very large south-facing window, as seen from a fixed observation point in the room. Each curve is for a different month (or pair of months where the curves are similar for two months). The straight lines are the time of day. The origin represents a viewpoint directly opposite the window at the level of the working plane. The diagram is presented at full size in the *Accessories* on page 95 where it is drawn to a scale of 1:100 for a viewpoint 2 m from the window. The circle on the diagram is a reminder of the distance to the viewpoint; its radius, 20 mm, is 2 m to this scale. The circle therefore also represents the view seen within a 90° cone from the viewpoint 2 m from the window.

Self-assessment exercise 5

1   What is the recommended duration of sun availability to occupants of buildings who may reasonably expect to receive sunlight?

2   Which of the following orientations for unobstructed windows will receive sufficient probable sunlight hours to meet the *BS Daylight Code*[2] recommendations for interiors, where the occupants have a reasonable expectation of direct sunlight?

- WNW
- ESE
- NNE

3   In what circumstances are blinds or other means of controlling sunlight most needed?

4   Low transmission glasses can reduce solar heat gain, sky glare and sun glare. True or false?

5   Will vertical fins mounted on a south-facing facade affect primarily the time of day or the time of the season of the year at which the sun penetrates? Draw a sketch to work this out.

6   An outline proposal for a college shows a 3-storey building with a central court or atrium about 12 m by 18 m. The client wishes to have this court daylit, with a reasonable quantity of light reaching the floor of the atrium, and with sun admitted in the winter but largely excluded in summer to avoid overheating. In this situation movable blinds are not thought advisable. Devise a scheme for the roof of the atrium, relying mainly on fixed external screening. A sketch or description of the main principles will suffice.

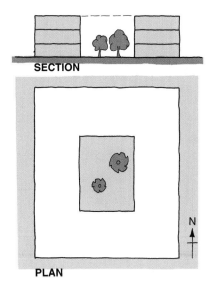

SECTION

PLAN

N

Answers on page 70

Summary of daylight design procedure

The design procedure summarised here is related to the RIBA *Plan of work*, stages A–E[9]. A more detailed design procedure not linked to the RIBA *Plan of work* is in the *CIBSE Window Manual* (pp 1–23)[3].

A Inception

Architect and building services engineer agree their respective responsibilities and the procedure for daylight design.

B Feasibility

Clarify aspects of the brief affecting daylighting, for example:

- what importance should be attached to the view out?
- what is the nature of visual tasks?
- is the building to be primarily daylit?
- will there be daylight exclusion zones?
- what are the normal occupation times?
- is there a need for privacy (preventing seeing in)?
- what are the ventilation needs?
- what are the energy targets and environmental objectives?

Record features of the site, nearby buildings and trees, etc likely to affect daylight, view, overshadowing, etc.

Obtain climatic and other environmental data for the site, for example probable daylight and sunlight hours and ambient noise levels.

Identify relevant standards and statutory requirements and local authority planning directives.

Consider planning and user needs affecting building depth, room height, number of storeys and orientation — for example:

- sizes of user groups such as classes in schools,
- proportion of activities not requiring daylight,
- nature of site and other constraints such as local authority planning directives and overshadowing of, or by, adjacent buildings.

Using rules of thumb based on view, average daylight factor and Building Regulations requirements, estimate the gross areas of windows and any rooflights.

Provide the information for initial cost estimates.

C   Outline proposals

Identify the main design options which meet the brief and daylighting needs.

Compare the performance of the options in terms of:

- views provided,
- modelling of interior,
- quantity and quality of daylight for tasks (combined where necessary with electric lighting),
- life costs.

Consider using model studies.

D   Scheme design

Develop the preferred design option as part of the building as a whole, assessing the:

- adequacy of the views provided,
- effect of the light flow through the interior and how it affects the surface illuminance and modelling,
- admission of sunlight and the need for shading devices,
- average daylight factor in relation to visual tasks and supplementary electric lighting where needed, including controls,
- quality of lighting, including colour rendering and avoiding glare,
- energy efficiency,
- structural considerations,
- external appearance of buildings.

For large buildings, consider using large-scale models (say 1:10 scale) of the main or most common spaces.

Refine the calculations (minimum daylight factor calculations may be needed in critical areas).

Make periodic checks of the capital and running cost implications of using daylight (eg window cleaning, supplementary electric lighting and maintenance).

Model box exercise

Why make models?

Models can be used in many fields of architectural design. Several of our more important buildings have had their lighting studied using models. The effects of light can be scaled, since they depend on geometry.

Most models used to design lighting are carefully detailed and crafted. But a simple shoebox can be used to demonstrate several of the principles of daylighting and the quality of light produced by the window. The average daylight factor gives broad guidance on the area of glass needed for a design, but it does not take into account the size and position of the window. It is these aspects of window design that this exercise sets out to explore.

The basic exercise

1 Preparing the box

Construct three windows in one side of the box — for each make a central vertical cut with horizontal cuts at the top and the bottom, see Figure 50. (This allows the window to be opened and closed as required. Drafting tape can be used to hold the flaps back.) The area of each end window should be half that of the central window. The windows should be central to the height of the box and roughly as shown in the diagram. Size the windows so that the three windows together are about half the area of the window wall.

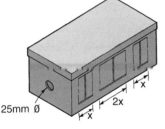

50 Shoebox model for examining the effect of windows on the quality of light

This allows you to model two different window combinations which admit the same quantity of light to the interior. These are:

- central window open and the end windows closed,
- end windows open and central window closed.

Cut a peep hole in one end wall of the box. Adjust the size of this hole (25 mm diameter works well for most people) so that you can see most of the interior. If you look into the peep hole, allowing sufficient time for adaptation to take place, and then vary the window arrangement, the lighting of the room changes, irrespective of the ambient lighting conditions. If the box is rotated through 90° onto its side, the windows become rooflights, see Figure 51. (Do this part of the exercise out of doors, not too close to a building.)

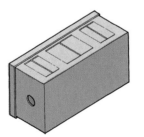

51 The model is rotated so that the windows become rooflights

2 Alternative window arrangements

Consider the four alternative arrangements in Figures 52–55 below.

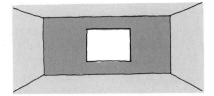

52 Side lit, single window

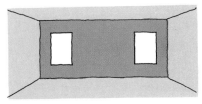

53 Side lit, two windows

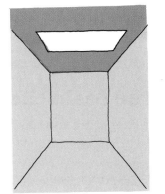

54 Top lit, single rooflight

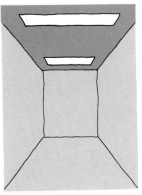

55 Top lit, two rooflights

3 Initial assessment

Take the box to a window, or preferably out of doors, where it can be studied by daylight. With the box side lit, you can now assess how well the model room appears to be lit. By changing from the single window to the two windows, you will see how the position of windows affects the appearance of the room.

Calculate the average daylight factor using the formula on page 30. Look into the model again to get an idea what this average daylight factor looks like.

4 Sketching what you see

To study these variations in detail, draw the view of the interior paying special attention to the pattern of light and shade. Draw it to a size no greater than A4 and use a soft pencil. Repeat this for each of the four conditions listed in step 2 above.

Assess your sketches as you progress. The sketch should be as accurate a representation of the model box interior as you can make it. Look particularly at the match of tones and the brightness pattern, especially towards the corners of the box.

5 Comparing your sketches

Put the sketches in pairs — the two side lit and the two top lit — as in Figures 52–55. Compare the light and shade patterns. Do you prefer one set of lighting conditions to the others. Why should this be so?

Do the pairs appear to be equally well lit? What do you mean by *well lit*? What aspects of the sketches help you to form this opinion?

Although the texture of the box material may not be pronounced, which lighting arrangement makes it more evident?

Which appears to be better lit, the side-lit pair or the top-lit pair? By how much?

Calculate the average daylight factor for the toplighting condition, noting that the visible sky angle is much larger than for a side window. Compare this calculated result with your subjective assessment.

Other ways of using the model

That is the basic exercise. You can repeat it under sunlight, or expand it by putting objects, such as the *haystack,* into the shoebox. Note the contributions and quality of light from different directions.

By moving to a different location, you can study the effects of different obstructions outside the windows.

If you make a rather larger model box, you can take photos inside it using a wide-angle lens, see Figure 56. (With an ordinary lens, the photo would include little else than the far end wall.)

Adapting the box further

You may like to add a second set of openings, in the top of the box, the same size as the windows you cut in the side of the box. This will allow you to compare lighting the *same space* with first windows and then rooflights. You will find that rooflights will give about twice as much daylight as the same area of windows.

The interior can be clad with two different coloured papers to study their effects on inter-reflections, or with textured papers.

The box can be developed further by replacing the window walls with other window arrangements. What is the effect if:

- the window area is in the form of a clerestory?
- the end windows are moved closer to the end walls?
- the window is shaped to make the best of the view?

Comparing the model with reality

At some stage during this exercise, you may wonder whether the principles noted in such a simple model study can be valid. Look in the real world for the things you observe in the model. Similarly, effects from the real world should be looked for in the model. (To explore this aspect, you could even make a further model of a real room you know.) This is an exercise aimed chiefly at developing perceptual abilities.

Window pattern	Internal appearance (photo of model)	Contours of illuminance

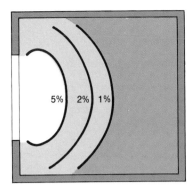

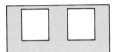

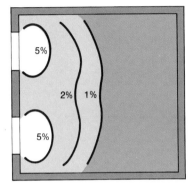

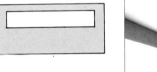

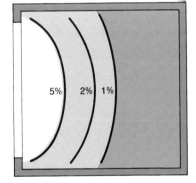

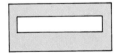

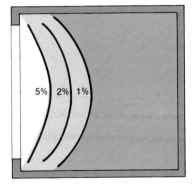

56 The effect of window pattern on the distribution of light and shadow in a room. The total area of window is the same in each case

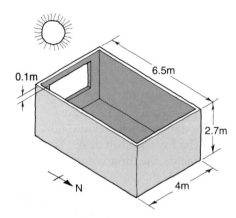

57 Dimensions of the room

Window design exercise

The brief

This is an exercise in designing the size, shape and position of a window in a small room. The room should have a predominantly daylit appearance; a good view is a priority.

Other assumptions and constraints for the exercise are as follows:

- the room is a general office with the dimensions shown in Figure 57, at latitude 53° north,

- the room has a white ceiling (reflectance 0.7), light walls (reflectance 0.5) and a typical floor (reflectance 0.3),

- there is a single double-glazed window,

- the window faces due south, is unobstructed and uses clear glass,

- the design should include a shading device to prevent sunlight penetrating more than 1 m into the room on the work surface between April and August,

- as the window is to be double-glazed, to save energy its area must not be more than 40% of the wall area unless compensating measures are taken (see *Building Regulations*[10]).

A photograph which has been taken of the fine unobstructed view from the site is in the *Accessories*, as are other design aids you will need for the exercise.

Approach and summary

Before carrying out this exercise in detail on pages 56–60, we outline here the numbered stages of the design process, summarising the results and conclusions as we go along — then discussing how the design must be revised to resolve any conflicts

Preliminary design

1 Maximum window area. The energy saving constraint demands that the area of the single glazed window must be at most 40% of the window wall. So we begin by calculating that area — we find it is 4.3 m².

2 Average daylight factor. As the room is to be predominantly daylit, the window must have an average daylight factor of at least 2%, and if possible 5% (from Table 6, page 31). For the window area of 4.3 m², using the formula on page 30, we find that the average daylight factor is 2.8%. This is adequate, but as it is less than 5% the Table tells us that some electric light will be needed to supplement daylight.

3 Depth of room. As our room is low, narrow and deep, we should also apply the formula for limiting depth on page 31. This tells us that our room is just within the limit.

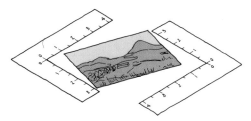

58 The L-shaped masks and the photograph of the view for choosing the position and shape of the window

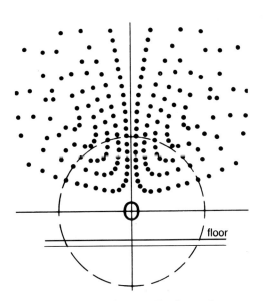

59 The pepperpot diagram. The dots each represent a patch of sky which contributes an equal amount of light (0.1% for direct light, 0.05% for light from an obstruction). The patches of sky are smaller at the zenith than the horizon because the zenith is brighter

4   *View*. As view is a priority, we must now decide where to place the window so that it frames the view in the photograph to the best advantage, see Figure 58.

5   *Sun penetration*. If the window is quite large, we may need to control sunlight. So next we superimpose the window outline on the south-facing sun path diagram, to discover for which months of the year the sun penetrates the room. We find that the sun penetrates the room for 3 or 4 hours during the summer months between April and August. To exclude the sun between April and August, as the brief requests, we could lower the head of the window below the April–August sun path, or we could add some kind of sun shade. To reduce the period of sun penetration each day, we could add vertical fins.

6   *Minimum daylight factor*. The average daylight factor only gave us an initial check on the area of glazing, and our depth formula suggested our room is at the limit for depth. So we should now check whether enough skylight will reach the least-well-lit desk. To do this, we calculate the minimum daylight factor, the three components of which were illustrated in Figure 21 (page 29).

If you do not have a computer daylight program, you can calculate the minimum daylight factor manually. To calculate the first two components of daylight factor — the sky component, and the externally reflected component — superimpose a drawing of your window on the pepperpot diagram in the *Accessories*, see Figure 59. Then calculate the internally reflected component from a formula, see page 60.

The daylight factor at the least-well-lit desk proves to be about 1.6%. This is well over half the average daylight factor of 2.8% we calculated earlier, so it is satisfactory.

Iteration — revising the design

To resolve any conflicting requirements, the design process outlined above will need to be iterative — adjusting the window and, if necessary, modifying some of your criteria.

For example, if you first chose to lower the window head or add a horizontal overhang to shield the viewpoint from the sun between April and August, this will obstruct daylight. But as the room is already at the limiting depth for daylight, you would then need to make it less deep, or accept larger electricity bills. Instead you may prefer to use a retractable blind or canopy.

Or, if you found that the area of the window is too small to do justice to the fine view, you may want to suggest triple glazing to your client. The Building Regulations allow larger windows if they are triple glazed. But the windows would then need to be a great deal larger, since triple glazing transmits about 20% less light than double glazing (Table 3, page 31).

As a further exercise, you could calculate the area of triple glazing needed to ensure an average daylight factor of 5% in this room. Do the new Building Regulations allow such a large percentage of window area — even with triple glazing? It would probably provide a generous view out. How would you propose to screen the sun? Methods of comparing the life costs of different types of glazing, taking into account energy consumption, are dealt with in another document, *Energy efficiency and lighting design*[1].

Detailed design

The previous section explained and summarised the steps involved in determining the size, shape and position of a window, and the iteration process that should follow the first round of calculations. We will now go through the steps again, looking more closely at those calculations.

1 Maximum window area

Building Regulations limit the net area of a double glazed window to 40% of the window wall:

$$40\% \ (4.0 \times 2.7) = 4.3 \ m^2$$

2 Average daylight factor

Apply the formula on page 31 to this window area of 4.3 m², making the following assumptions:

- transmittance T = 0.65 (0.9) = 0.59, for clear double glazing in a clean location (0.9) — from Table 3,

- the visible sky angle Θ is almost 90º as the view is unobstructed,

- the average reflectance of all the internal surfaces (A), which are light, is about R = 0.5 — from Table 2.

We now calculate the total internal area of the room, and then the average daylight factor itself:

$$A = 2 \ (6.5)(4.0) + 2 \ (6.5 + 4.0) \ 2.7 = 109 \ m^2;$$

$$\overline{D} = \frac{W}{A} \ \frac{T\Theta}{(1 - R^2)} \ = \ \frac{4.3}{109} \ \frac{0.59(90)}{1 - (0.5)^2} \ = \ 2.8\%$$

3 Depth of room

As our room is low and narrow, but deep, we can apply the formula for limiting depth (page 31)

$$\frac{L}{w} + \frac{L}{h} \ \leq \ \frac{2}{(1 - R_b)}$$

Left side: $\dfrac{L}{w} + \dfrac{L}{h} \ = \ \dfrac{6.5}{4} + \dfrac{6.5}{2.6} \ = \ 4.1$

Right side: $\dfrac{2}{(1 - R_b)} \ = \ \dfrac{2}{(1 - 0.5)} \ = \ 4$

So the room is approximately at the limiting depth for daylighting — a fraction over.

$$\overline{D} = \frac{W}{A} \ \frac{T\Theta}{(1 - R^2)}$$

where:

$\overline{D}$ = average daylight factor

W = window area (using Table 5 to correct for framing)

A = area of all surfaces of the room in m² (floor, ceiling, and walls including windows)

T = glass transmittance (from Table 3) corrected for dirt (using Table 4)

Θ = visible sky angle — see Figure 23

R = average reflectance of area A (from Table 2)

Average daylight factor formula from page 30

$$\frac{L}{w} + \frac{L}{h} \ \leq \ \frac{2}{(1 - R_b)}$$

where:

L = depth of room from window to back wall

w = width of room measured across the window wall

h = height of window head above floor

R_b = area-weighted average reflectance in the back half of the room (the value for a typical office is likely to be around 0.5)

Formula for limiting room depth from page 31

4 View

Use the landscape photograph and the two L-shaped masks from the *Accessories*. Design your window to enclose the portion of the view you want to be seen from a given point in the room, using the instructions on the masks — Figure 60.

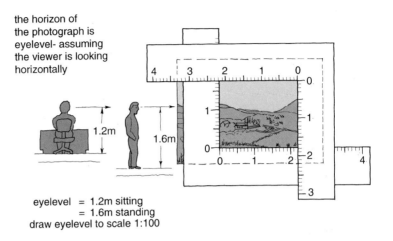

the horizon of the photograph is eyelevel- assuming the viewer is looking horizontally

1.2m

1.6m

eyelevel = 1.2m sitting
= 1.6m standing
draw eyelevel to scale 1:100

60 Designing your window to suit the view

The two white masks are marked with a grid with 0.1 m divisions to a scale of 1:25. For a viewpoint at the centre of the room and a little over 3 m back from the window, you can read off the actual size of your chosen window by counting the grid divisions directly. (A note on the masks explains how to deal with other viewing distances and positions.)

Check that your chosen window does not have a larger area than the maximum we calculated earlier — W = 4.3 m².

5 Sun penetration

Use the south-facing sun path diagram for latitude 53° north from the *Accessories*. Figures 61–63 describe how you can use this diagram to predict the months and times of day when the sun will penetrate the window to your chosen viewpoint. Figure 64 then uses this analysis to design a sunshade.

Internal curtains and blinds are more effective at reducing sun glare than in reducing solar heat gain. This is because they and the glass heat up and warm the room.

The effect of vertical fins can be assessed in a similar way to that shown for canopies in Figure 64 (by projecting from the sun path diagram onto a plan of the room). Generally, for southerly facades, canopies reduce the season during which sun can penetrate, whereas fins control the time of day when the sun can penetrate. Controlling sun penetration for specific times of day or season is most difficult for south-easterly or south-westerly windows; for these orientations, diagonal louvres are an effective means of control.

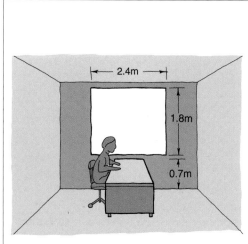

61 The window to be tested

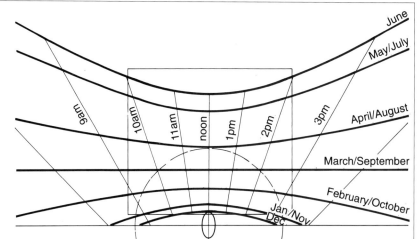

62 Drawing your window on the sun path diagram

The brief called for sunlight to be prevented from penetrating more than 1 m from the window on the work surface between April and August.

When you draw the window on the sun path diagram (Figure 62) the scale at which you draw it depends on the distance of your viewpoint from the window.

This is part of the south-facing sun path diagram for latitude 53° north from the sets in the *CIBSE Window manual*[3]. The diagram was explained on page 45. Draw the window on a copy of the sun path diagram, with the origin at the working plane height and opposite the viewpoint (centred on the window in this case). As our viewpoint is 1 m from the window, we should ideally use a sun path diagram twice the scale — but we can use the same sun path diagram if, instead, we draw the window to a scale twice as large, ie 1:50. Read off the sun penetration: for example in June the sun penetrates from before 10 am to after 2 pm; in February and October from about 8.30 am to after 3.30 pm.

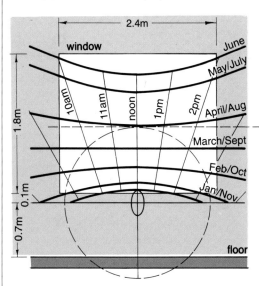

63 Predicting sun penetration

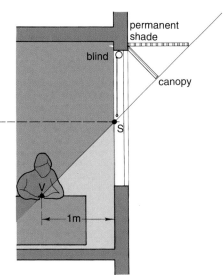

64 Designing a sunshade

This illustration repeats the centre part of Figure 62. To exclude the sun from the viewpoint, 1 m from the window between April and August, the lower edge of the shading device needs to just obscure the April–August sun path. Project this lower edge across to intersect the plane of the window at S on the section through the room in Figure 64.

The lower edge of the shade must reach down to the line through V (viewpoint) and S (intersect). The section in Figure 64 shows various options for creating this shade.

A permanent shade would reduce the daylight all year, in effect increasing the depth of the room, which is already at the limiting depth (page 31). So a retractable blind or canopy would be a better choice.

61–64 Predicting sun penetration and designing a sunshade

6 Minimum daylight factor

Assuming that there are filing cabinets at the back wall, the least-well-lit desk is likely to be about 4 m from the window wall and against the side wall. This gives us a viewpoint 4 m back and about 1.5 m from the centre line of the window.

Daylight factor is made up of three components that must be calculated separately. They were defined in Figure 21 (page 29).

$$\text{Daylight factor} = SC + ERC + IRC$$

Sky component (SC)

We use the pepperpot diagram to discover what percentage of the total skylight reaches our viewpoint. It is drawn to a scale of 1:100 for a viewpoint 2 m back from the window wall; the 20 mm circle on the diagram reminds us of this. As our viewpoint is twice as far from the window (4 m instead of 2 m), it will see less sky (fewer dots) than from 2 m. So we must draw the window proportionally smaller, in the ratio 2 m/4 m — ie, to a scale of 1:200. See Figure 65.

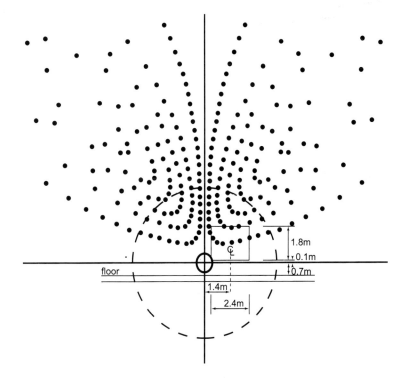

65 Draw the window on the pepperpot diagram to the scale 1:200. This is half the normal scale, since the viewpoint is twice the usual distance

The centre line on the pepperpot diagram represents the point directly opposite the viewer. As our viewpoint is 1.4 m offset from the centre of the window, we centre our window 1.4 m from the centre line of the pepperpot diagram. That gives an offset of 7 mm at the scale of 1:200.

We draw the window so that the origin on the diagram is at the working plane level (0.7 m for an office).

Counting the dots within the outline of the window, you will find there are about 8. As each dot contributes 0.1% of daylight:

$$SC = 8\,(0.1\%) = 0.8\%$$

If there had been obstructions to the view, we should have drawn these onto the window as they would be seen from the viewpoint. Then discount any dots covered by the obstruction, and count these later as the externally reflected component.

Externally reflected component (ERC)

As there are no obstructions in this case, ERC = 0.

(Ground reflections are calculated approximately within the IRC formula, not as ERC)

Internally reflected component (IRC)

To calculate IRC, we use the following formula from page 29 of the *CIBSE Window manual*[3]:

$$\text{IRC} = \frac{0.8 \; W}{A(1-R)} \; (C \, R_{fw} + 5 \, R_{cw}) \; (\%)$$

where:

W	=	the net glazed area of the window (m^2)
A	=	the total area of the ceiling, floor and walls, including windows (m^2)
R	=	the area weighted average reflectance of the interior surfaces (A)
R_{fw}	=	the average reflectance of the floor and those parts of the walls (excluding the window wall) below the plane of the mid-height of the window
R_{cw}	=	the average reflectance of the ceiling and those parts of the walls (excluding the window wall) above the plane of the mid-height of the window
C	=	a coefficient having values between 0 and 39 depending on the angle of the obstruction above the horizon. The *CIBSE Window manual* (p 29 table B1.2)[3] gives values of C for different angles of obstruction. For no obstruction, C = 39.

$$\text{IRC} = \frac{0.8 \; (4.3)}{109 \; (0.5)} \; (39 \, (0.4) + 5 \, (0.6))$$

$$= 1.17\%$$

Convert this from average to *minimum* IRC by multiplying by 0.78, a factor which varies depending on room reflectance (*BS Daylight Code*[2], Appendix A, Table 3, page 27):

$$0.78 \; (1.17) \; = \; 0.81\%$$

Add the three components

Adding the three components above together, the minimum daylight factor at the least-well-lit desk is:

$$(SC + ERC + IRC) \; = \; (0.8 + 0 + 0.81) \; = \; 1.61\%$$

Answers

Answers to *Twenty questions* (page 6)

1   Windows are:

   - for view

   - to enhance the appearance of interiors

   - for the illumination of visual tasks.

   Windows also can provide a convenient means of natural ventilation.

2   *Daylight* is the combination of *skylight* and *sunlight*. Sunlight is the direct beam from the sun. Skylight is daylight without sunlight.

3   There is guidance in the *BS Daylight Code*[2], page 12, clause 8.2 *Overshadowing*, and more fully in the BRE Report: *Site layout planning for daylight and sunlight; a guide to good practice*[11].

4   The maximum areas of glazing in walls and roofs are specified in relation to energy conservation in the *Building Regulations* 1995 Part L[10], and in the *Building Standards (Scotland) Regulations 1990*[12]. Window positions and sizes may have to be restricted to prevent fire spread to adjacent buildings. The requirements are summarised in *BS Daylight Code*[2], page 15, clause 11.3. (Regulations are modified from time to time so please check latest revisions.)

5   *Possible sunlight hours* are those when the centre of the sun is above the horizon, though it may be obstructed by clouds. *Probable sunlight hours* is the long-term average of the total number of hours in which direct sunlight reaches unobstructed ground (ie after obstruction by clouds is taken into account).

6   The *working plane* is the plane — whether horizontal, vertical or inclined — on which the visual task lies. If no precise information is available, the working plane may be taken, for design purposes, to be 0.7 m above floor level for offices and 0.85 m above floor level for industry.

7   False. Reflectance is a measure of the ability of a surface to reflect light. A glossy surface would reflect its light in a different way from a matt surface, but — given the same reflectance — the total amount of light reflected will be the same.

8   Factors contributing to the deterioration of fabrics, paints and other materials include:

   - the spectral composition of the light (blue and ultra-violet wavelengths are usually the most harmful),

   - the illuminance (for very sensitive materials the illuminance should not exceed 50 lux),

   - the length of exposure.

   Further information is given in the *BS Daylight Code*[2], page 14, clause 10.

9   No. For lighting design purposes the term *overcast* implies 10/10ths cloud cover, and this applies to the whole sky. When skylight illuminance is to be calculated, a term is included in the formula to account for the higher illuminance from the south on non-overcast days.

10 The *daylight factor* is a ratio of the illuminance at a point within the room, to the illuminance on a horizontal plane outdoors under an overcast sky. It is used to calculate or to measure the adequacy or otherwise of daylight at a *given point*, for example, for a particular task.

The *average daylight factor* is the mean daylight factor over a horizontal working plane. It is used as the measure of general daylight illumination and may be related to the subjective assessment of the adequacy of daylight in the interior.

11 The recommendations in *BS Daylight Code*[2] for the minimum values of average daylight factor in dwellings are:

- bedrooms — 1%
- living rooms — 1.5%
- kitchens — 2%.

12 True.

13 Four basic forms of control that can be linked to daylight are:

- manual
- timed switch-off, with optional manual reset
- sensors that determine whether or not a space is occupied
- photo-electric switching — on/off.

14 Factors to be considered include:

- daylight should appear to be dominant (this will probably mean an average daylight factor of 2% or more)
- colour rendering under each light source should be similar
- the effect of modelling from side windows should be maintained
- surfaces surrounding windows can be brightened by electric light, to reduce glare
- lighting controls need to be designed so that people will switch off lights when they are not needed.

15 Supplementary electric lighting might be needed to improve the distribution of illuminance so that:

- visual tasks have good light
- the contrast between the window wall and the view outside is reduced
- the overall appearance of the interior is enhanced.

16 False. They are excluded.

17 The **window** *reference point* should not be confused with the **room** *reference point*:

plane of inside surface
of window wall

window
reference
point

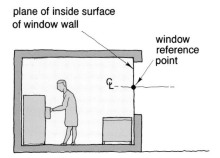

The **window** *reference point* is the point in the centre of the window or rooflight opening, lying on the plane of the inside surface of the window wall or roof. It is used when determining hours of sunlight penetration, average daylight factor and the internally reflected component.

typical room
reference points

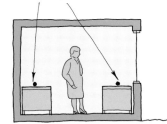

A **room** *reference point* is a point in an interior (usually on the working plane) for which the daylight factor is being calculated. It is not a unique point in the room.

18 The deepest penetration into an interior will be from either the east or the west because of the low angle of the sun at these orientations. The southern sun is always at greater altitude. Southern sunlight will penetrate deeper into the room in winter than summer.

19 *Disability glare* impairs vision to such an extent that visual performance is seriously affected, for example where a chalkboard in a classroom has to be viewed next to a bright window. The classic example is the disability caused by oncoming car headlights on an otherwise unlit road. *Discomfort glare* causes discomfort and, perhaps, some impairment of visual performance.

20 Yes, in England and Wales, although generally a period of 20 years uninterrupted access and enjoyment may be necessary to establish such a right. No such legislation applies to Scotland. Further information is given in *BS Daylight Code*[2], page 14, clause 11.2.

Answers to exercise 1: *View* (page 21)

1   A view from a window has these benefits:

- it gives contact with the outside, and with the variety provided by the changing weather, seasons and time of day
- it contrasts with the interior scene
- it provides a visual rest centre — a change of focus for the eyes
- it prevents claustrophobic feelings
- it helps one orientate oneself within the building.

The order of importance differs from person to person, but most people would rate the first point above as the most important one.

2   Because the area of the view visible through the window from the back of a deep room will be less.

3   By day, lace and net curtains, although reducing the amount of daylight entering a room, give privacy in a room while allowing a view out. From outside the curtains are well illuminated by day. This prevents people from seeing through them to the dimmer room beyond. By night, the situation is reversed if the lights in the room are switched on. Compare this effect with that of open weave scenic cloth found in theatres, which appears to melt away when the back stage lighting is brought up. Such effects obviously vary with the openness of the weave and the relative brightnesses either side of the curtain.

4   The area is 2.16 m² (ie, 20% of 2.7 m × 4 m)

5   A large room which offers internal views of at least 15 m can allow the eye muscles to relax, even though the windows in the external walls are too far away to provide a view meeting *BS Daylight Code*[2] recommendations.

Smaller rooms which have no external walls can have glazed openings in partitions (preferably larger than the minima in Table 1 on page 18) giving onto a larger shared space. It may be possible to provide this larger shared space with rooflighting that can give some of the variety offered by windows, eg changing skylight and splashes of sunlight. This is the atrium found in many large commercial buildings today. But note that occupants of small rooms that just look into larger rooms which have external windows seem to feel more deprived.

Indoor planting, or even fountains, can be used to give some of the assets of being able to view a scene outdoors, but these require continuous, careful maintenance.

Visual stimulus and interest can be provided in interior rooms by variations in brightness brought about by appropriately designed electric lighting, interior decoration and colour schemes.

Consider people's need for privacy, as overlooking — staring — can be more frequent and less anonymous than from out-of-doors into a building.

Place desks or work stations so that the maximum number of people can see a window, even if distant.

Answers to exercise 2:
Appearance of interiors (page 27)

1 The wall near the window would receive light from the wide angle of the window and so the texture would be softened. The rear wall would receive light head-on, flattening its texture. At the rear of the side walls, the light strikes at grazing angles and the texture would be pronounced.

2 The window head should be as high as possible to take advantage of the brighter part of the sky towards its zenith, and to see the sky above any obstruction opposite.

3 The patterns of light and shade will be altered to some extent; shadows may be softened and the wall surrounding the main window will be partially lightened, reducing the contrast with the view.

4 By using *contrast grading*. If the head, sill or jamb of the window can be near, respectively, to the ceiling, floor or a return wall, light reflected from any of these surfaces will brighten the window surround and thus reduce contrasts. Deep or splayed jambs will grade brightnesses viewed from the inside; likewise light coloured frames and glazing bars.

5 Yes. Please carry out one of the model box exercises described on page 50, with the points in this section particularly in mind, and using the *haystack* from the *Accessories*.

Answers to exercise 3:
Daylight and skylight (page 35)

1   In working interiors, daylight can provide:

- adequate levels of illumination for much of the year, particularly in buildings up to 14 m deep overall,
- good modelling of the task,
- stimulating variation in the brightness of surfaces through the day,
- good colour rendering,
- energy savings.

2   The *no-sky line* is an imaginary line joining points on a plane in the interior from which the sky can no longer be seen. The area beyond this line receives no direct skylight and so relies on reflected light for its illuminance. The point from which the sky can no longer be seen has also been called the *grumble point*. (But note that the phrase *grumble point* is also used, *with a different definition*, as a legal term in cases of right to light.)

3   By the *daylight factor*, which is the ratio, expressed as a percentage, of:

- illuminance at the point on the working plane indoors,

divided by:

- illuminance due to an unobstructed hemisphere of the sky.

Direct sunlight is excluded from both measurements.

4   Glare from windows can be minimised by:

- detailing the window surrounds to improve *contrast grading*, eg by splaying the jambs, using light coloured frames;
- brightening the surrounding wall surfaces with light coloured finishes, cross-lighting from other windows or electric lighting (where it is used during the day);
- using adjustable blinds;
- using external canopies and fins.

Note that the last two methods will also reduce the quantity of daylight entering the room.

5   Use the formula for *average daylight factor* on page 30:

$$\overline{D} = \frac{W}{A} \ \frac{T\Theta}{(1 - R^2)}$$

Where:
   $\overline{D}$ = average daylight factor
   W = 2.16 m² within the frame
   A = 88.6 m²
   T = 0.80 (0.9) = 0.72, for single (0.80), clean (0.9) glazing
   Θ = about 90° as there are no obstructions opposite, and
       assuming there is no projection above the window
   R = 0.5 assuming light internal surfaces

so:
$$\overline{D} = \frac{2.16}{88.6} \ \frac{0.72(90)}{1 - (0.5)^2} = 2.1\%$$

So, to give a daylit appearance, supplementary electric lighting will be needed (see Table 6 on page 31).

6   Use the formula for *limiting depth* on page 31:

$$\frac{L}{w} + \frac{L}{h} \ \leq \ \frac{2}{(1 - R_b)}$$

Where:
   L = 5 m
   w = 4 m
   h = 2.7 – 0.7 = 2 m
   R_b = 0.5 for a typical light office.

So the left side of the equation is:

$$\frac{L}{w} + \frac{L}{h} = \frac{5}{4} + \frac{5}{2} = 3.75$$

The right side of the equation is:

$$\frac{2}{(1 - R_b)} = \frac{2}{(1 - 0.5)} = 4$$

As 3.75 < 4, the room just passes the limiting depth rule.

7   For *single* glazing, there is no need to calculate the whole formula again. Multiply the answer to question 5 above by the ratio (new window area)/(old window area)

$$\overline{D} = \frac{35\%}{20\%} (2.1) = 3.7\%$$

For *double* glazing, the transmittance drops from 0.80 to 0.65 (from Table 3 page 30). So

$$\overline{D} = \frac{0.65}{0.80} (3.7) = 3\%$$

Note: the window area is now 35%/20% (2.16) = 3.78 m²

8 To give an *average daylight factor* of 5% with double glazing, increase the window area in the proportion 5%/3% (where 3% and the area 3.78m² comes from the last answer). So:

$$W = \frac{5\%}{3\%}(3.78) = 6.3 \text{ m}^2$$

The higher the head of the window, the better the skylight will be. So place the head, say, 0.2 m from the ceiling.

The window should be tall enough to allow both seated and standing people to see views of close as well as distant objects. So place the sill close to the level of the working plane — say with the glass starting at 0.8 m.

So the height of the window is 2.7 – (0.2 + 0.8) = 1.7 m and the width must be 6.3/1.7 = 3. 7 m.

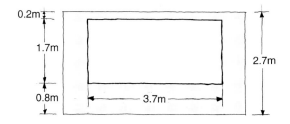

Answers to exercise 4:
Daylight with electric light (page 39)

1   When the average daylight factor is below 2%, the contribution from daylight to task illumination is considered to be negligible and work should be regarded as lit by electric light alone.

2   Lamps which have an *Intermediate class correlated colour temperature* and are screened from the view of occupants.

3   The fittings could be arranged in rows parallel to the window wall and the switching devised to provide electric lighting in areas remote from the windows of about the same illuminance as that of typical daylight levels 2 m from the window. (This is not a precise recipe.) The method of control will depend on the type of occupancy and the hours of use.

Answers to exercise 5: *Sunlight* (page 47)

1 The *BS Daylight Code*[2] recommends (page 8, clause 5.3) that sunlight should be received for 25% of probable sunlight hours. Between 23 September and 21 March this reduces to 5%.

2 ESE. (WNW and NNE face more than 90° from due south.) See the rule of thumb in Figure 35.

3 Sunlight needs to be controlled:
- where overheating is likely, ie where the annual penetration of sunlight exceeds one-third of *probable sunlight hours* (*BS Daylight Code*[2], footnote to page 8),
- in working interiors where people cannot readily move their working positions, and
- where interiors contain materials liable to fade in direct sunlight.

4 True. However, the intensity of the sun is so great that, even if reduced to one-tenth of its original intensity, it would still cause disability glare.

5 Vertical fins can be used to control the time of day that the sun is allowed to penetrate — see the sketch in the margin. Horizontally edged overhangs can be designed to control the season of the year when the sun penetrates.

6 Various schemes could meet this brief — for example:
In summer the low altitude sun, from the east in the early morning and the west in the evening (A in the sketch below), could be excluded by vertical fins. The high altitude sun in the middle of the day (B) could be excluded by transverse louvres, angled to admit the low altitude winter sun (see the sketch below).

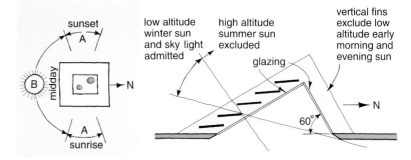

If this array was set on a glazed roof with a 30° pitch facing south, the other side, at a 60° pitch facing north, would admit little or no sun (vertical fins could be provided if required) but would admit most of the skylight for the atrium throughout the year. The shading devices will, of course, affect the quantity of skylight admitted.

An alternative solution using similar external arrays could be based on a factory-type monitor roof — see the sketch below. The geometry of these rooflights can be checked using the procedure on pages 57–58, using the sunpath diagram in the *Accessories*.

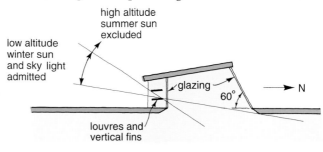

References and further study

References

1 RIBA and CIBSE open learning project on lighting and design. A series of four packages:

  - 6/1 Light, perception and architecture: introduction to a refresher course, by Karen Paxton and John Kay
  - 6/2 Designing buildings for daylight, by James Bell and William Burt
  - 6/3 Designing electric lighting in buildings, by Joe Lynes
  - 6/4 Energy efficiency and lighting design, by Kevin Mansfield

  Obtainable from: Education Department, RIBA, 66 Portland Place, London, W1N 4AD, and CIBSE, 222 Balham High Road, London, SW12 9BS.

2 **British Standards Institution.** Code of practice for daylighting. *British Standard* BS 8206:Part 2:1992. London, BSI, 1992.

3 **The Chartered Institution of Building Services Engineers.** *Applications manual: Window design.* London, CIBSE, 1987.

4 **Slater A I and Davidson P J.** *Energy efficient lighting in buildings.* A Thermie Programme Action. Garston, Building Research Energy Conservation Support Unit, BRE, 1992.

5 **British Standards Institution.** Code of practice for energy efficiency in buildings. *British Standard* BS 8207:1985 (pp 6 and 7, Section three, Economic analysis). London, BSI, 1985. Also Amendment No 1 to BS 8207:1985; *Amendment* AMD 8151, February 1994.

6 **The Chartered Institution of Building Services Engineers.** *Code for interior lighting.* London, CIBSE, 1994.

7 **British Standards Institution.** Code of practice for artificial lighting. *British Standard* BS 8206:Part 1:1992. London, BSI, 1992.

8 **Building Research Establishment.** Lighting controls and daylight use. *BRE Digest* 272. Garston, Construction Research Communications, 1983.

9 **Royal Institute of British Architects.** *Plan of work.* RIBA, 1983.

10 **Department of the Environment and the Welsh Office.** *The Building Regulations Approved Document L. Conservation of fuel and power* (1995 edition). London, HMSO, 1994.

11 **Littlefair P J.** *Site layout and planning for daylight and sunlight: a guide to good practice.* Building Research Establishment Report. Garston, Construction Research Communications, 1991.

12 *The Building Standards (Scotland) Regulations 1990.* Statutory Instrument 1990 No 2179 (S 187). London, HMSO, 1990.

Further reading

BRE publications

Building Research Establishment. Estimating daylight in buildings 1. *BRE Digest* 309. Garston, CRC, 1986.

Building Research Establishment. Estimating daylight in buildings 2. *BRE Digest* 310. Garston, CRC, 1986.

Crisp V H C, Littlefair P J, Cooper I and Mckennan G. *Daylighting as a passive energy option: an assessment of its potential in non-domestic buildings.* Building Research Establishment Report. Garston, CRC, 1988.

Hunt D R G. *Availability of daylight.* Building Research Establishment Report. Garston, CRC, 1979.

Littlefair P J. Daylight design for display-screen equipment. *Building Research Establishment Information Paper* IP10/95. Garston, CRC, 1995.

Littlefair P J. Daylight sunlight and lighting control. *Building Research Establishment Teaching package.* Garston, CRC, 1994.

Littlefair P J. Measuring daylight. *Building Research Establishment Information Paper* IP23/93. Garston, CRC, 1993.

Littlefair P J. Site layout for sunlight and solar gain. *Building Research Establishment Information Paper* IP4/92. Garston, CRC, 1992.

Littlefair P J. Innovative daylight systems. *Building Research Establishment Information Paper* IP22/89. Garston, CRC, 1989.

Littlefair P J. Average daylight factor: a simple basis for daylight design. *Building Research Establishment Information Paper* IP15/88. Garston, CRC, 1988.

Littlefair P J. Solar dazzle reflected from sloping glazed facades. *Building Research Establishment Information Paper* IP3/87. Garston, CRC, 1987.

For further details of these BRE publications and how to obtain them, see the back cover.

Other publishers

Anstey J. *Rights of light and how to deal with them.* London, Royal Institution of Chartered Surveyors, 1988.

Clarke H W, Nelson J and Thompson E. *Knight's Building Regulations.* London, Charles Knight, 1986.

Commission of the European Communities. *Daylighting in Architecture* A European Reference Book, Edited by N Bailer, A Franchiotti and K Steemers. James and James Ltd, 1993.

Department for Education and Science. Guidelines for environmental design and fuel conservation in educational buildings. *Design Note* 17. London, DfE, 1981.

Ellis P. *Rights to light.* Estates Gazette, London, 1989.

Evans B H. *Daylight in architecture.* London, McGraw-Hill, 1981.

Environmental Advisory Services. *Solar heat gain through windows.* Environmental Advisory Services Report (Pilkington Bros Ltd) (1981).

Lam W. *Sunlight as formgiver for architecture.* New York, Van Nostrand, 1986.

Lynes J, Burt W and Marsden M. *Hyperlight* (a hypertext open-learning database on lighting and energy). Available from the Hyperlight Partnership, 4 Aigburth Avenue, St Georges Road, Hull, HU3 3QA.

Further study opportunities

The journals of the RIBA, CIBSE, and some lighting companies offer a ready way of furthering your interest in lighting.

Reference should also be made to CIBSE publications. There are Guides on many specific areas of lighting, such as hospital and health care buildings, lecture theatres and spaces containing visual display terminals.

The RIBA and CIBSE both offer sessional meetings to which visitors are welcome. Also, they can arrange contact with organisations providing mid-career courses (Continuing Professional Development) in lighting.

Pages 71 and 72 list several recent relevant publications which will provide more information on specific areas of the subjects raised in this document. In turn, they will refer to other publications — unfortunately many of the classic books they refer to are now out of print, although their content is still largely valid.

Local colleges and university libraries are likely to have a wide selection of books, including out-of-print material. While such libraries are mainly for the use of present and past students, it is worth trying to get temporary access if the local library cannot obtain wanted books. Direct contact with the local school of architecture may be profitable.

The National Illumination Committee, which can be contacted through CIBSE*, is the link with international activities in lighting. It organises periodical meetings specifically on daylight, and can obtain CIE publications.

There are courses available at many universities, and also several part-time courses.

---

* CIBSE is at 222 Balham High Road, London SW12 9BS.

Appendices

Appendix A

Statutory requirements

Here we summarise recent requirements but these are in the process of being superseded by European directives.

General

The Offices, Shops Railway Premises Act 1963.

The Health and Safety at Work etc Act 1964.

Rights of Light

The Prescription Act 1832 (for England, Wales and Northern Ireland).

The Rights of Light Act 1959 (for England and Wales).

The Rights of Light Act 1961 (Northern Ireland).

The Rights of Light Acts apply only to the countries mentioned and require that there be an uninterrupted period of twenty years' access and enjoyment to establish such a right.

These acts are described as enabling acts — they state only that light shall be suitable and sufficient for the performance of activities. It is generally accepted that lighting which meets the current version of the *CIBSE Code for Interior Lighting*[A1] will comfortably meet both of these requirements, though the legal entitlement to light is much lower than this.

Building Regulations

Department of the Environment and the Welsh Office. *The Building Regulations Approved Document L. Conservation of fuel and power (1995 edition)*. London, HMSO, 1994.

The Building Standards (Scotland) Regulations 1990. Statutory Instrument 1990 No 2179 (S 187). London, HMSO, 1990.

Statutory Instruments

Specific requirements apply under Statutory Instruments to particular activities (such as schooling, food processing, the manufacture of luminaires), but, in general, they concentrate on electric lighting.

There is neither legal right to, nor legal guidance on, sunlight or view.

Note. See also the section in the *BS Daylight Code* (pp 14, 15)[A2] on statutory requirements affecting the provision of daylight.

References to Appendix A

A1 **The Chartered Institution of Building Services Engineers.** *Code for Interior Lighting*. London, CIBSE, 1994.

A2 **British Standards Institution.** Code of practice for daylighting. *British Standard* BS 8206:Part 2:1992. London, BSI, 1992.

Appendix B

The energy-saving potential of daylight

This is a partial summary of a BRE Report, *Daylighting as a passive solar energy option*[B1]. For a fuller discussion of the energy-saving potential of daylighting, see the companion volume on lighting and energy efficiency[B2].

Potential energy savings

Early studies suggested that energy consumption was least with low or zero glazing areas. But this work generally focused only on minimising heat-losses, neglecting the energy consumed by the lighting system and the loss of solar heat. The current view is that daylighting is a valuable means of improving the energy efficiency of buildings, especially non-domestic buildings such as offices, schools, factories, and hospitals.

For example, where appropriate switching controls have been installed in offices, so that lights are only used when necessary, daylighting has often reduced the energy spent on artificial lighting by as much as 40%. A further finding from a number of studies reported by BRE[B1], is that a building's window area can often be varied over a relatively wide range (centred on about 50% of the building facade) without greatly affecting its total energy consumption. As the window area increases, solar gain increases and less energy is needed for lighting, compensating for the increase in heat-losses through the larger windows.

But energy will only be saved on lighting if people turn off lights when they are not needed — something which they rarely do. To be sure lights are only on when needed, new forms of lighting control are usually needed. One example is centrally controlled time-switching to put all lights off at lunch time, coupled with local switching so that only people who need the light switch it on after lunch.

As the amount of energy a building uses need not be greatly affected by the area of glazing (for the reasons explained above), visual criteria can be allowed to play an important part in window design, provided the controls for switching the lights are suitable.

References to Appendix B

B1 Crisp V H C, Littlefair P J, Cooper I and McKennan G. *Daylighting as a passive solar energy option: an assessment of its potential in non-domestic buildings.* Building Research Establishment Report. Garston, CRC, 1988.

B2 *Energy efficiency and lighting design* (see page 71, Reference 1).

Appendix C

Credits for illustrations

The ink and wash drawings on pages 1 and 43 were drawn by Gareth Slater

The graphics were devised by the book's authors and editors

Photographs

Page	Building	Figure No	Architect	Photographer
Cover	Zweifalten Abbey, Biberach, Baden-Wurttenberg, Germany	–	J M Fisher	James Bell
3	St Dominic's, Rotterdam	–	–	James Bell
4	Barons Hall, Penshurst Place, Kent	1	–	Michael Wheeler (Photo courtesy of Trustees of Penshurst Place)
4	Banqueting Hall, Whitehall, London	2	Inigo Jones	Valerie Bennett (Photo courtesy of Architectural Association)
4	Woollen Mill, Nailsworth, Glos	3		Eric de Maré
4	Fred Olsen Amenity Centre, Millwall Docks, London	4	Foster Associates	Richard Einzig
7, 8, 9	Offices at Wilmslow	–	BDP	William Burt
7, 10, 11	House at Wilmslow	–	James Wareham	William Burt
7, 12, 13	Burrell Collection art gallery, Glasgow	–	Barry Gasson	Jeremy Preston, Barry Gasson, William Burt
7, 14, 15	Maths building, Westgate School, Winchester, Hampshire	–	Hampshire County Architect's Office	Derek Phillips
17	House at Grindleton, Lancs	–	Tom Mellor	James Bell
18	Greenhead High School, Huddersfield	6	Development Group, Department for Education and Science	John Kay
22	House at Chipperfield, Herts, 1936	8	Maxwell Fry	Derek Phillips
22	House at Rickmansworth, Herts, 1937	10	Connell, Ward and Lucas	Derek Phillips
23	Entrance gallery, Residenz, Munich	11	–	James Bell
23	Tower Thistle Hotel, London	12	Howard Renton	James Bell
23	Schoenbrunn Palace, Vienna	13	–	John Kay
24	Library, Architectural Association, Bedford Square, London	14	–	William Allen
24	St Anne's College, Oxford	15	Howell, Killick, Partridge and Amis	Sydney W Newberry (left) Richard Einzig (right)
26	Bentalls, Kingston-upon-Thames	16	BDP	Derek Phillips
26	Harlequin Centre, Watford	17	Chapman, Taylor	Derek Phillips
26	The Ark, Hammersmith, London	18	Ralph Erskine	Rupert Truman

Continued overleaf

Photograph credits continued

Page	Building	Figure No	Architect	Photographer
26	St Enoch Centre, Glasgow	19	Unknown	Alastair Hunter (Photo courtesy of GMW Partnership)
28	Factory	—	Unknown	William Burt
36	TSB regional headquarters	—	Unknown	William Burt
40	County Offices, Winchester, Hants	32	Hampshire County Architect's Office	Derek Phillips
40	House at Bovingdon, Herts	33	Derek Phillips	Derek Phillips
41	House at Bovingdon, Herts	34	Derek Phillips	Derek Phillips
42	Police Support HQ, Eastleigh, Hants	40	Hampshire County Architect's Office	Derek Phillips
42	W H Smith, Greenbridge offices, Swindon	41	Ahrends, Burton & Koralek	Unknown
44	Model of classroom in artificial sky	47	—	William Allen
53	Views inside model room	56	William Burt's model	William Burt
83, 88	Landscape view for exercises	—	—	Timothy Bell

Appendix D

List of artificial skies in the UK

Artificial skies are available for use at a number of establishments throughout the UK. Most of the information in Appendix D is taken from: **Littlefair P J and Lindsay C R T**, Scale models and artificial skies in daylighting studies, *BEPAC Technical note* 90/3, 1990; available from BEPAC, David Bartholomew Associates, 16 Nursery Gardens, Purley on Thames, Reading, RG8 8AS, telephone and fax 01734 842861.

As the survey shows, many of the laboratories have other facilities such as mock-up rooms or photometric equipment which are available for hire, usually at modest fees. The staff concerned often have considerable expertise in daylight issues and are usually willing to give advice if required.

Organisation	Type of sky	Fee and services	Other equipment
Architectural Association, London.	No artificial sky		
Bartlett School of Architecture 22 Gordon Street, **London**, WC1H 0QB. Mr D Loe/Mr K Mansfield 0171 387 7050	Mirror CIE overcast 3 m × 3 m	Fee charged Assistance available	Artificial sun, heliodon, wide range of photometric equipment
School of Architecture and Civil Engineering University of Bath, Claverton Down, **Bath**, Avon, BA2 7AY. Mr A Wilkinson 01225 826826 (SB) 01225 826941 (DL)	Mirror CIE overcast 4 m × 4 m	Fee charged Assistance available	Heliodon, miscellaneous lighting equipment and mock-up facilities
Department of Mechanical Engineering Brunel University, **Uxbridge**, UB8 3PH. Dr B E Smith 01895 27400 x 2880	Mirror CIE overcast 2 m × 2 m	Fee charged Assistance available	Heliodon, illuminance and luminance measuring instruments
Building Research Establishment Garston, **Watford**, WD2 7JR. Dr P Littlefair 01923 664874 Fax: 01923 664782	Mirror CIE overcast 4 m × 4 m	Fee charged Assistance available	Heliodon, mock-up room, wide range of photometric equipment, artificial sun
Department of Architecture, School of the Built Environment, De Montfort University, The Gateway, **Leicester**, LE1 9HB. Dr K Lomas 01116 275 7445 Fax: 01116 257 7449	Mirror CIE overcast 2.4 m × 2.4 m	No fee Assistance available	Heliodon, solarscope, photometric equipment
Department of Building Engineering and Surveying, Heriot Watt University Riccarton, **Edinburgh**, EH14 4AS Mr R Webb 0131 449 5111 x 4619	Mirror CIE overcast 1.7 m × 1.7 m	Nominal fee charged Assistance available	Heliodon, rotating house 8.5m × 8.5m for daylight studies, wide range of photometric equipment
Centre for Architecture, School for the Built Environment, Liverpool John Moores University, 98 Mount Pleasant, **Liverpool** L3 5UZ. Dr N Sturrock 0151 231 2121 (SB) 0151 231 3705 (DL)	Mirror CIE overcast 1.5 m × 1.5 m	Fee negotiable Assistance available	Heliodon, photometric instruments, mock-up room 7m × 3.5m
The Martin Centre, 6 Chaucer Road **Cambridge**, CB2 2EB. Dr N Baker or Dr K Steemers 01223 332981 Fax: 01223 332983	Mirror CIE overcast 2.4 m × 2.4 m	Fee charged Assistance available	Heliodon, photometric instruments
School of Construction, Sheffield Hallam University, Pond Street, **Sheffield**, S1 1WB Mr P Ward 01742 532019 Prof R Mackenzie 01742 533217, main SB 01742 720911	Mirror CIE overcast 2 m × 2 m	Fee charged Assistance available	Photocells

Continued overleaf

List of artificial skies in the UK (cont)

Organisation	Type of sky	Fee and services	Other equipment
South Bank University, Borough Road **London**, SE1 0AA. Mr J Love 0171 815 7651 or 01585 281279 (mobile)	Mirror CIE overcast 1.6 m × 1.6 m	Fee charged Assistance available	Photometric instruments, mock-up rooms
School of Architecture and Building Engineering, University of Liverpool, P O Box 147, **Liverpool**, L69 3 BX Dr D Carter 01151 794 2622 (DL) Fax: 01151 794 2605	Mirror CIE overcast 2.5 m × 2.5 m dimmable	Assistance available	Photometric instruments, motorised heliodon, model building service
Dept of Building Engineering, UMIST, P O Box 88, **Manchester**, M60 1QD. Dr G Levermore 0161 200 4257	Mirror CIE overcast 1.5 m × 1.5 m	Fee charged Assistance available	Heliodon, luminance meters, lux meter
Building Science Section, Dept of Architecture, University of Newcastle-upon-Tyne, **Newcastle**, NE1 7RU Prof T J Wiltshire 0191 222 6007	Mirror CIE overcast 3 m × 3 m	Fee charged Assistance available	Heliodon, photometric instruments, model building service
Low Energy Architecture Research Unit (LEARN), Dept of Architecture and Interior Design, University of North London, 166–220 Holloway Road, **London**, N7 8DB. Mr M Wilson 0171 753 7006 Fax: 0171 753 5780	Dome CIE overcast 3.6 m diameter mirror CIE overcast 2.4 m × 2.4 m	Fee charged Assistance available	Heliodon, photometric instruments
Dept of Architecture, University of Nottingham, University Park, **Nottingham**, NG2 7RD. Dr J Whittle 01602 513170	No longer have artificial sky		Artificial sun
Building Science Research Unit, School of Architectural Studies, University of Sheffield, **Sheffield**, S10 2TN Pof P Tregenza 01742 824707 (DL)	Mirror CIE overcast 2 m × 2 m	Fee charged Assistance available	Heliodon, daylight coefficient measuring device, sky scanner, model building service, mock-up space
Department of Building, University of Ulster, Jordanstown, Newtownabbey, **County Antrim**, BT37 0QB Dr G McCullagh 01232 365131	Artificial sky disassembled		
Welsh School of Architecture R & D, UWCC, Bute Building, King Edward VII Avenue, **Cardiff**, CF1 3AP. Mr M Parry 01222 874000 x 5981 or x 4018 Fax: 01222 874192	Mirror CIE Overcast 1.5 m × 1.5 m	Fee charged Assistance available	Heliodon, photometric instruments
The Faculty of the Built Environment University of the West of England, **Bristol**, Frenchay Campus, Coldharbour Lane, Bristol, BS16 1QY. Mr P Innocent 01117 656261 x 3021, fax: 01117 763895	Mirror CIE Overcast 1.2 m × 1.2 m	Fee charged Assistance available	Heliodon, photometric benches, illuminance meters and luminance meters
Anglia Polytechnic University Design & Communications Systems, Victoria Road South, **Chelmsford**, Essex, CM1 1LL	Mirror CIE Overcast 3 m × 3 m	Fee charged Assistance available	Heliodon, range of photometric equipment, computer program
Birmingham School of Architecture Perry Bar, **Birmingham**, B42 2SU Miss L J Heap 0121 331 5106	Mirror CIE Overcast 2.4 m × 2.4 m	Fee charged Assistance available	Heliodon, photometric instruments
University of Westminster, London	No longer has an artificial sky		

Appendix E

Definitions

Average daylight factor (see also Daylight factor)
Average indoor illuminance on a horizontal plane, as a percentage of the simultaneous outdoor illuminance from the unobstructed sky. (For a more precise definition, see the *BS Daylight Code*, reference 2 page 72.)

CIE standard overcast sky
(Commission Internationale de l'Eclairage)
A completely overcast sky for which the ratio of its luminance (L_γ) at an angle of elevation (γ) above the horizon to the luminance (L_z) at the zenith is given by the formula:

$$L_\gamma = \frac{L_z (1 + 2 \sin \gamma)}{3}$$

Daylight
Combined sunlight and skylight.

Daylight factor
Ratio, expressed as a percentage, of illuminance at a point on the working plane indoors, divided by the illuminance measured simultaneously outdoors on a horizontal plane due to an unobstructed hemisphere in the sky. (For a more precise definition, see the *BS Daylight Code*, reference 2 page 72.)

No-sky line
The outline on a given surface of the area from which no sky can be seen.

Externally reflected component
Ratio, expressed as a percentage, of that part of illuminance at a point on a given plane that is received directly after reflection from external obstructions under a sky of assumed or known luminance distribution, to illuminance on a horizontal plane due to an unobstructed hemisphere of this sky.

Illuminance (compare with luminance)
The luminous flux density at a surface, ie the luminous flux incident per unit area (lm/m^2 or lux). This quantity was formerly known as the illumination value or illumination level.

Internally reflected component
Ratio, expressed as a percentage, of that part of illuminance at a point on a given plane that is received after reflection from interior surfaces under a sky of assumed or known luminance distribution, to illuminance on a horizontal plane due to an unobstructed hemisphere of this sky.

Luminance (compare with illuminance)
The SI unit of brightness ($cd\ m^2$) measured by the luminous intensity of the light emitted or reflected in a given direction from a surface element, divided by the area of the element in the same direction.

Obstruction
Anything outside a building which prevents a direct view of the sky from a given reference point.

Possible sunlight hours

The total number of hours during the year in which the centre of the sun is above the unobstructed horizon.

Probable sunlight hours

The long-term average of the total number of hours during the year in which direct sunlight reaches the unobstructed ground.

Room reference point

The point in an interior for which the daylight factor is calculated (see the illustration on page 63).

Skylight

Part of solar radiation that reaches the earth's surface as a result of scattering in the atmosphere.

Sky component

Ratio, expressed as a percentage, of that part of illuminance at a point on a given plane that is received directly from a sky of assumed or known luminance distribution, to illuminance on a horizontal plane due to an unobstructed hemisphere of this sky.

Note: Sunlight, whether direct or reflected, is excluded from all values of illuminance.

Solar altitude

Angular height of the sun above the horizon.

Solar azimuth

Horizontal bearing of the sun measured in degrees, either in a clockwise direction from north or in relation to due south.

Sunlight

That part of solar radiation that reaches the earth's surface as parallel rays after selective attenuation by the atmosphere.

Supplementary electric lighting

Electric lighting used continuously in combination with daylighting.

Window reference point

The point in the centre of a window or rooflight opening on the plane of the inside surface of the window wall or roof. This is used in determining sunlight penetration, average daylight factor, and the internally reflected component (see the illustration on page 63).

Working plane

Horizontal, vertical or inclined plane in which a visual task lies.

Note: if no information is available, the working plane may be considered to be horizontal and 0.7 m above the floor for offices; horizontal and 0.85 m above the floor for industry.

Appendix F

About the accessories

List of accessories

The accessories consist of the following items, referred to in the main text at the page given in brackets.

- Photograph of landscape view (p 54)
- Haystack (p 52)
- L-shaped masks for sizing windows for view (p 57)
- Window-wall templates, for view (p 20)
- Pepperpot diagram (p 55)
- Sunpath diagram (p 45)

Photo of view from the office

Photo of a landscape view

The landscape view has been taken with a 28 mm wide-angle lens on a 35 mm single lens reflex (SLR) camera and printed at the commercial size of 160 mm by 110 mm. To a scale of 1:25, a photo this size represents the view through a transparent window 4 m wide by 2.7 m high when the observer is 3.14 m back from the window wall.

The L-shaped masks described overleaf are scaled specially for use with this photo. (Note: most cameras used for family photos do not have a 28 mm wide-angle lens.)

The haystack

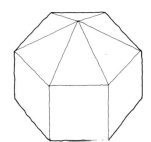

Haystack

The haystack is a simple device which is used to show the modelling effects of light and shadow patterns at any particular point within a space.

By comparing the brightness of each facet you can assess such things as the major flow of light, and the impact of secondary sources such as the effect of reflected light.

You can use it in the model box exercise (page 50) and also in real rooms.

L-shaped masks for sizing windows for view

This technique has been developed to allow an initial assessment to be made of view, window size and proportion, sky factor and sunpaths for distant views. The L-shaped masks are scaled specially for use with the landscape photo in the pack.

The white faces of the two L-shaped masks are marked with a grid with 0.1 m divisions to a scale of 1:25. For a viewpoint at the centre of the room and a little over 3 m back from the window, you can read off the actual size of your chosen window by counting the grid divisions directly.

For a viewing distance twice as large (about 6 m), use the grey faces of the masks with 0.2 m divisions to a scale of 1:50. For other distances, use the same recipe to adjust the scale. For example, to double the viewing distance again (to about 12 m), double the value of each division again — to 0.4 m — and work to a scale of 1:100.

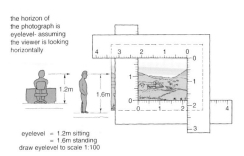

the horizon of the photograph is eyelevel- assuming the viewer is looking horizontally

eyelevel = 1.2m sitting
= 1.6m standing
draw eyelevel to scale 1:100

L-shaped masks for sizing windows for view

Instructions for using the L-shaped masks

Cut two L-shaped masks from the sheet (or make a photocopy on card and cut that up).

1. Use these masks only with a photo taken with the type of camera described on page 83.

2. Adjust the masks to frame the view you want.

3. Note the width and height of the window opening from the masks.

4. Check that the area of the window gives the required daylight (see page 30).

5. Place your chosen window on your window wall, so that the horizon in the view is at the occupants' eye level:
   - 1.2 m above ground level for a seated occupant, and
   - 1.6 m above ground for a standing occupant.

6. Check that the position chosen for the head of the window is below the level of the ceiling.

Note: a worked example is given on page 57.

Window-wall templates — for view

There are two sets of templates.

- Templates A, B, C, D have windows with areas 20% of the window wall. This is the minimum area recommended by the *BS Daylight Code*[F1] for view windows in rooms not more than 8 m deep.

- Templates E, F, G, H have windows with areas 40% of the window wall. (This is the maximum area set by the *Building Regulations Part L* (L1, Table 2) for offices and similar non-domestic buildings[F2].)

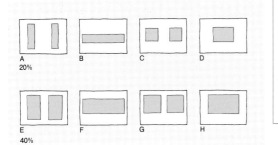

A | B | C | D
20%

E | F | G | H
40%

Window-wall templates

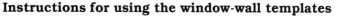

Instructions for using the window-wall templates

1 Make copies of the window-wall templates, cut round the walls, and cut the windows out of the walls.

2 Superimpose each template in turn on the landscape photo, or on other photographs of your own. Consider how effectively each window (or pair of windows) forms the view.

The pepperpot diagram

We can use the pepperpot diagram to calculate what percentage of the total skylight reaches a chosen viewpoint in a room through a given window.

Each of the dots in the pepperpot diagram represents a patch of sky which contributes an equal amount of light. For direct light, each dot contributes 0.1% towards the daylight factor; for light reflected from an obstruction, each dot contributes 0.05%.

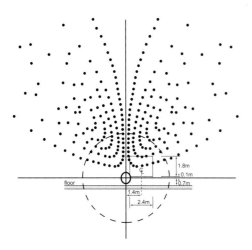

Pepperpot diagram

Instructions for using the pepperpot diagram

1 Decide the distance of your viewpoint from the window wall. This determines the scale at which you draw your window on the diagram. For example:

Distance to viewpoint	Scale of drawing
2 m	1:100
4 m	1:200
8 m	1:400

2 Decide the offset of your viewpoint from the centre line of the window.

3 Decide the height of the working plane above floor level (0.7 m for offices, 0.85 m for dwellings).

4 Draw your window on a copy of the pepperpot diagram to the scale given in the table above, using notes 2 and 3 above to locate it on the diagram. Also, draw on any obstructions as they will be seen through the window.

5 *Sky component.* To calculate the direct component of daylight factor, count the dots within the window which are not covered by obstructions. Divide these by 10 to get the sky component.

Externally reflected component. To calculate the component reflected from obstructions, count the number of dots covered by the obstructions within the window. Divide by 20 to get the externally reflected component.

Note: the internally reflected component is computed from a formula (given on page 60), not from the pepperpot diagram.

The pepperpot diagram is drawn to a scale of 1:100 for a viewpoint 2 m back from the window wall — the 20 mm radius circle on the diagram reminds us of this. So you can use it for other viewpoint distances by drawing the window to a different scale.

Sunpath diagram

The sunpath diagram is just one sample sheet drawn from the sets provided in the folder at the back of the *CIBSE Window manual*[F3]. This particular one is for a south-facing room at latitude 53° north, in the Midlands. The other sunpath diagrams in the set for this latitude are for other orientations — west, south-west, south-east, etc. There are also other sets for other latitudes; for example Edinburgh is latitude 56° north; London is between latitude 51° and 52° north.

The CIBSE sunpath diagram uses the gnomonic projection. The curve labelled June on the diagram is the path the sun traces out in mid-June on a vertical window 2 m from a viewpoint at working-plane level. The other curves are for other times of year. The diagrams are drawn to a scale of 1:100 — see Figure 49.

The straight lines intersecting the sunpaths are time lines. For example, the 11.00 line connects the points on all the sunpath curves which the sun reaches at 11.00 GMT.

Sunpath diagram

Instructions for using the sunpath diagram
Full instructions are given in the worked examples in Figures 61–64.

A key aspect is choosing the correct scale to draw the window on the diagram. The diagram is drawn to a scale of 1:100 for a viewpoint 2 m from the window. But for other distances to the viewpoint, adjust the scale as follows.

Distance to viewpoint	Scale of drawing
1 m	1:50
2 m	1:100
4 m	1:200

References to Appendix F

F1 **British Standards Institution.** Code of practice for daylighting. *British Standard* BS 8206:Part 2:1992. London, BSI, 1992.

F2 **Department of the Environment and the Welsh Office.** *The Building Regulations Approved Document L. Conservation of fuel and power (1995 edition).* London, HMSO, 1994.

F3 **The Chartered Institution of Building Services Engineers.** *Applications manual: Window design.* London, CIBSE, 1987.

Accessories

Contents

Photograph of landscape view

Haystack

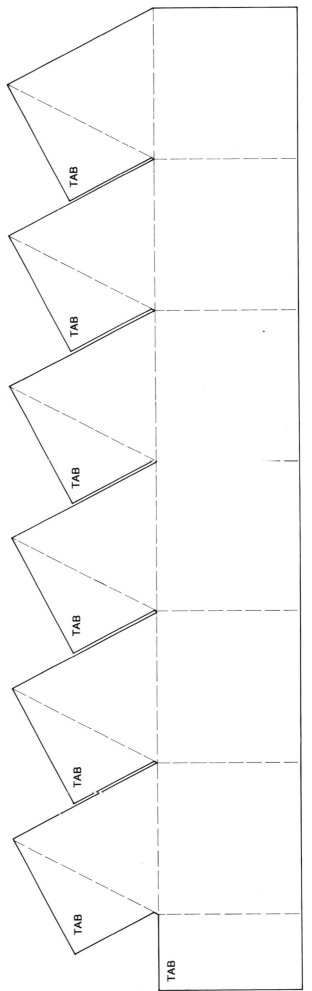

Cut along solid lines.
Score and fold along broken lines.
Glue tabs.
Assemble as shown.

L-shaped masks for sizing windows for view

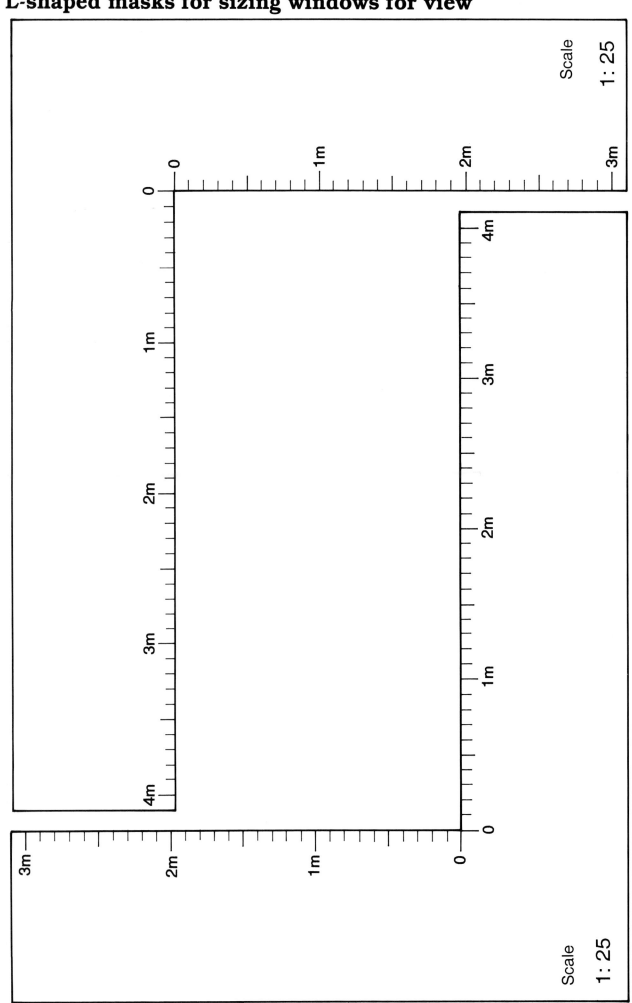

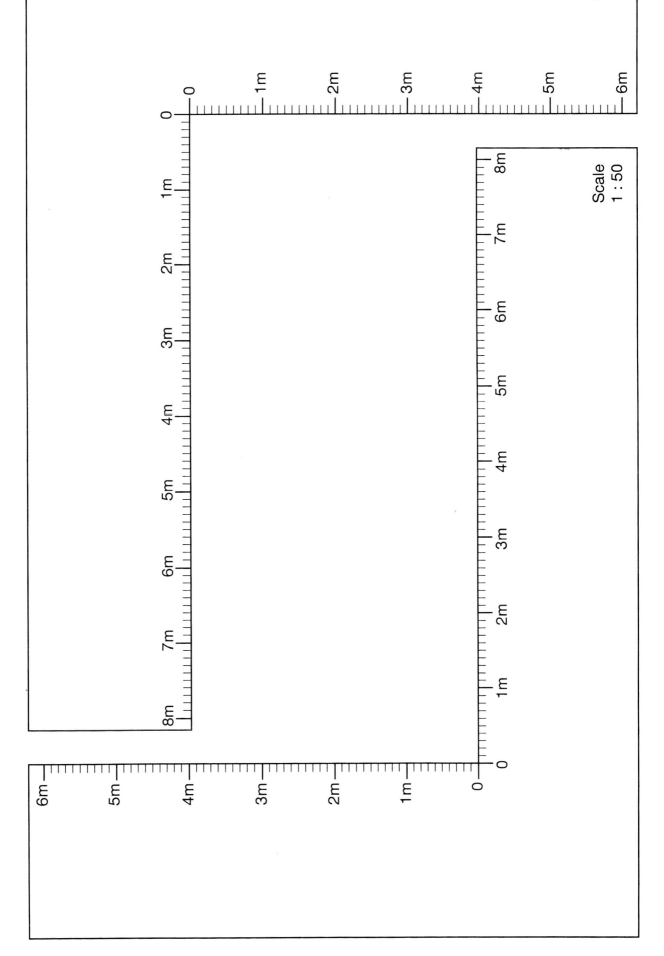

Scale
1 : 50

Scale
1 : 50

0
1m
2m
3m
4m
5m
6m

0
1m
2m
3m
4m
5m
6m
7m
8m

8m
7m
6m
5m
4m
3m
2m
1m
0

6m
5m
4m
3m
2m
1m
0

Window-wall templates, for view

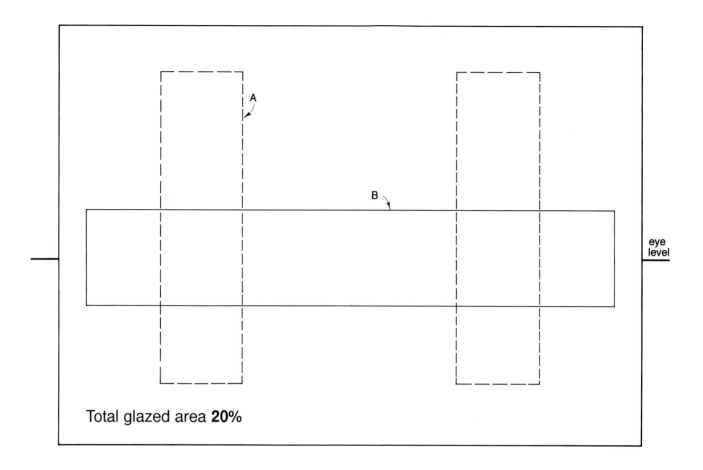

Total glazed area **20%**

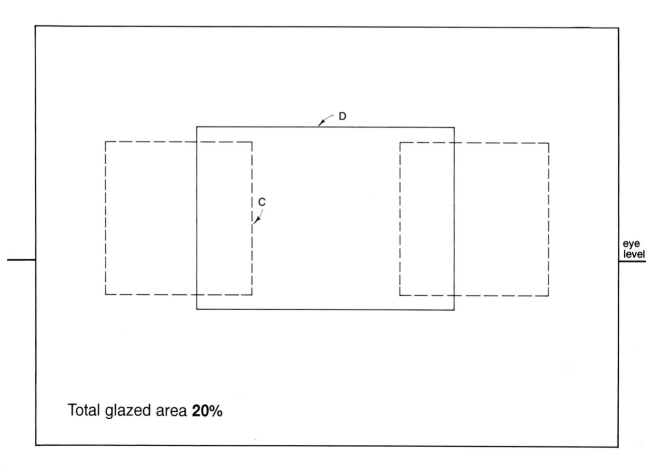

Total glazed area **20%**

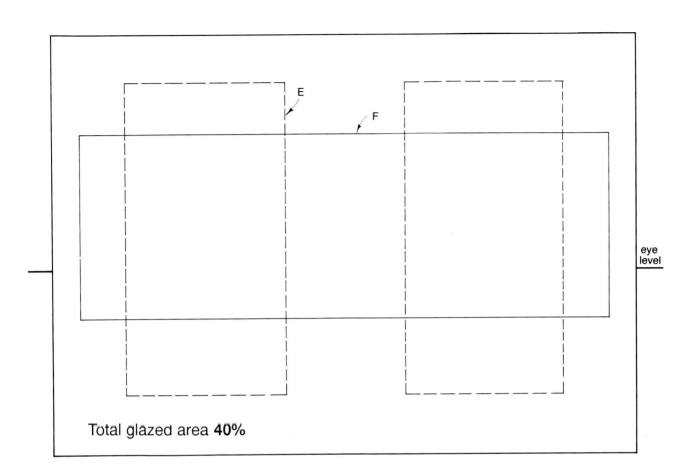

Total glazed area **40%**

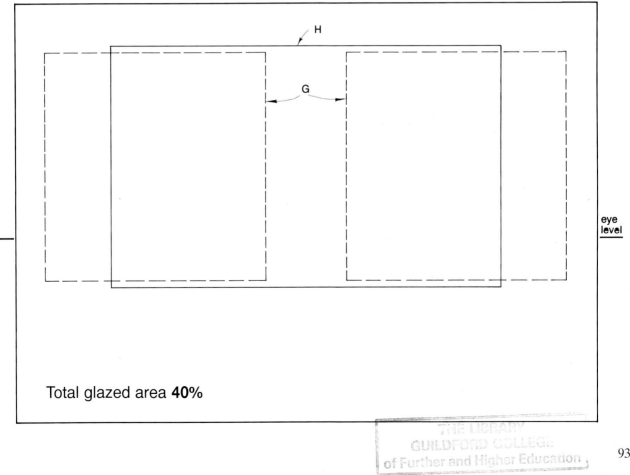

Total glazed area **40%**

Pepperpot diagram

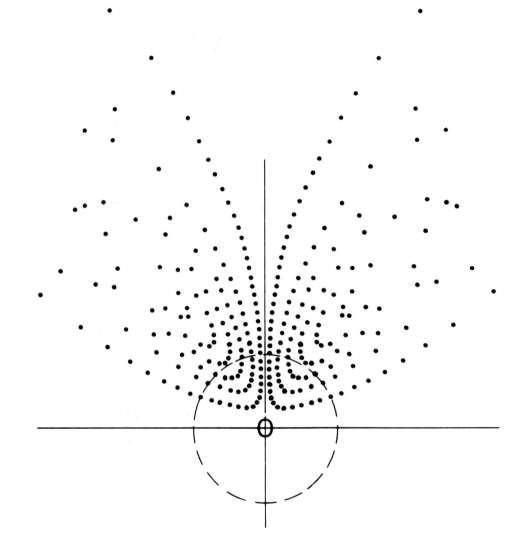

Sunpath diagram

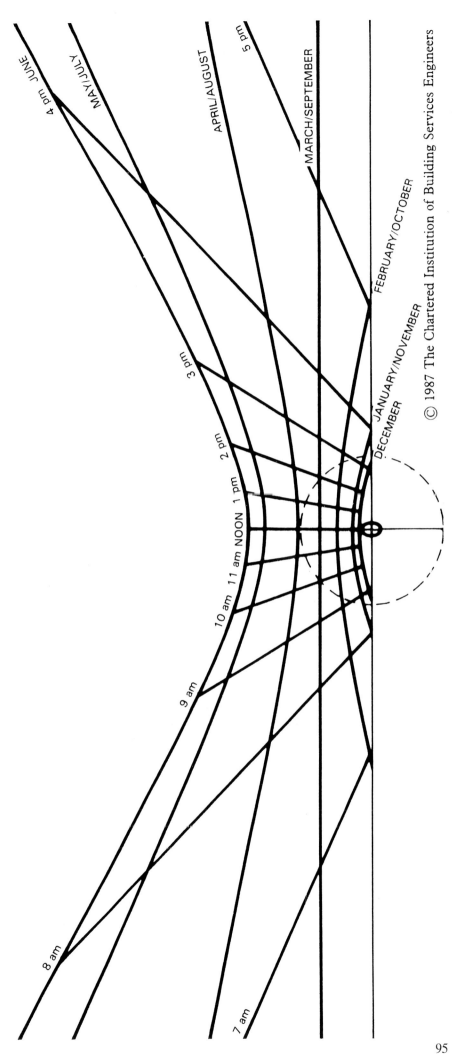

© 1987 The Chartered Institution of Building Services Engineers